ETERNAL ECHOES

Erich Neumann's Timeless Relevance to Consciousness, Creativity, and Evil

Nancy Swift Furlotti, PhD

Zurich Lecture Series in Analytical Psychology

ISAPZURICH

Volume 10

CHIRON PUBLICATIONS • ASHEVILLE, NORTH CAROLINA

www.ChironPublications.com

Interior and cover design by Danijela Mijailovic
Printed primarily in the United States of America.

ISBN 978-1-68503-163-3 paperback
ISBN 978-1-68503-164-0 hardcover

Library of Congress Cataloging-in-Publication Data Pending

CONTENTS

Erich Neumann
1905-1960

Courtesy of the Erich Neumann Estate

In memory of
Erel Shalit

ACKNOWLEDGEMENTS

First of all, I would like to acknowledge Erel Shalit, my partner, friend, and co-founder of the company we set up, Recollections LLC. Our collaborative work on a number of important books began with our co-edited book, *The Dream and its Amplification*, while we continued pursuing our desire to publish *Analytical Psychology in Exile: The Correspondence of C. G. Jung and Erich Neumann*. Our shared interest then focused on translating and publishing *Jacob and Esau,* and *The Roots of Jewish Consciousness, Volumes One and Two*. Erel's memory and inspiration has supported me throughout the writing of this book.

Additionally, I would like to thank many friends and acquaintances who were instrumental in my giving shape to the Neumann manuscripts, leading up to the publication of this book. Firstly, I appreciate the trust that was given to me and Erel by Erich Neumann's children, Micha Neumann, MD and Rali Neumann-Loewenthal, to bring the project of the correspondence between Erich Neumann and C. G. Jung to fruition, and then to translate and publish *Jacob and Esau* and *The Roots of Jewish Consciousness, Volumes One and Two*. Both saw the importance of their father's work and supported our vision to make these unpublished manuscripts available to the world.

I wish to thank Ann Lammers for the beautiful job she did editing and translating the difficult manuscript *The Roots of Jewish Consciousness* into English. Thanks goes to Tamar Kron and David Wieler for their translation of the original German manuscript into Hebrew, making it available in Erich Neumann's own land. The many conversations about the concepts, resources, and challenges that needed solutions in working with this material enriched my understanding of it and appreciation for its importance. It was from those experiences that I decided to pull together a synopsis of Erich Neumann's opus. Drawing from: his books *Depth Psychology and the New Ethic, The Origins and History of Consciousness, The Great Mother, Amor and Psyche, The Fear of the Feminine;* all his books on creativity including *Creative Man* and *The Child*; his essays "Mass Man," "Narcissism," and "Mystical Man"; and early manuscripts, *Jacob and Esau* and *The Roots of Jewish Consciousness*, my intention was to create a concise resource stimulating further interest and exploration in this Great Man's life work.

There were so many others who contributed to my understanding of Erich Neumann and his ideas. Dvora Kuchinski, who was in supervision with Neumann and a good friend of his for years, has been a rich resource through her stories and writings; Rina Porat, my deeply thoughtful and kind friend, has extensive knowledge of Neumann's work and I learned from listening to her and reading her well-written papers; Henry Abramovitch, who has an enduring interest in Erich Neumann's works and has written many interesting articles on his books; Riccardo Bernardini at The Eranos Foundation, has been particularly helpful when I had questions regarding Neumann or his many presentations there; and of course, Erel Shalit's interest and understanding of Neumann's material, evident in his own many books and conferences he helped organize on Erich Neumann. A special thanks goes to Murray Stein who encouraged me to present a workshop on the subject of Erich Neumann at the Zurich Lecture Series in 2022, and gave me the opportunity to publish this book. Finally, a big thank you goes to Steve Buser, Len Cruz and Jennifer Fitzgerald at Chiron Publications who have taken on this project and many before it. They have been impeccable in their oversight. To my copy editor Brooke Losey, I thank her for her sharp and careful eye in polishing my manuscript for publication. I could not be in better hands.

CHAPTER I
Introduction: Who is Erich Neumann?

Erich Neumann was a protégé and good friend of C. G. Jung. Thirty years younger, he was intellectually challenging, creatively building on and advancing Jung's works. His work, in many ways, deepened the understanding of Jung's. Explaining his understanding and observations of Jung's work, Neumann formulated many ideas and concepts of his own. Neumann's work clarified details not fully explained by Jung's emphasis on the archetypal and symbolic, especially regarding personal psychology and early stages of development. Jung was mostly interested in the second half of life, the process of individuation, and the transcendent function that leads to wholeness of the personality. He referred patients to Toni Wolff and Emma Jung who needed to first focus on the earlier or personal stages of development. Neumann's work filled in the gaps in understanding the development of the personality across the life-span.

Erich Neumann was born in Berlin, Germany in 1905. He was the third child of a successful grain merchant and raised in a well-to-do assimilated Jewish family. His higher education took place during the Weimar cultural period, which included a daring and spirited sensibility alongside economic insecurity and rising political tension. During his college years he studied philosophy, pedagogy, literature and Semitic studies. He pursued graduate study at the University of Erlangen in Nuremburg in philosophy, where he received his Ph.D. in 1927. With an interest in Hasidism and Kabbalah, Neumann wrote his dissertation on Arnold Kanne, a Christian philosopher-poet of the Romantic period influenced by Jewish Mysticism. Neumann then entered Medical School at Friedrich Wilhelm University in Berlin. Following his interests in the collective unconscious and the work of Jung and Sigmund Freud, Neumann intended to become a psychoanalyst. He passed his exams in 1933—the same year Germany implemented its Jewish race laws—making it impossible for Neumann to obtain an internship in order to practice. Years later, the University granted him his medical degree. With an interest in the arts, Neumann wrote poetry and a novel, *The Beginning*, and in 1932 undertook his study of Franz Kafka's stories.

Seeing the writing on the wall of what was developing in Germany, he and his wife Julie Blumenfeld, who he met at age 15, left to immigrate to Palestine along with their one-year-old son Micha. On the way, they moved to Zurich, Switzerland where they each entered analysis: Erich with Jung and Julia with Toni Wolff. A few months later, Julia and Micha went on ahead to Palestine while Erich remained behind to continue his analysis with Jung for a total of six months. He then followed and settled with his family in Tel Aviv where he lived for the rest of his life. He died there in 1960 at the age of 55 from kidney cancer. Jung, his good friend and colleague, died six months later in June of 1961.

Arriving in Palestine in 1934, Neumann was faced with a very difficult situation. He spent the war isolated from other Jungians and the vibrant intellectual community to which he was accustomed in Germany. One of Neumann's close friends growing up, Gerhard Adler, moved to London and also became a prominent Jungian analyst. Adler was a founding member of the Society of Analytical Psychology there. They remained friends throughout their lives. Neumann had an early but unpleasant encounter with Jungian analyst James Kirsch, who had arrived shortly before Neumann, but then left Palestine for London not long after his arrival. Kirsch went on to California, where he was one of the founders of the C. G. Jung Institute of Los Angeles. With all his admiration for Zionism, ultimately Kirsch could not tolerate the isolation from Europe and roughness of the country. Neumann was on his own in a new uncertain land. He focused his attention on what was happening in Europe, the unleashing of evil, and on finding his own Jewish roots. He started from the bottom, exploding with feelings regarding what was happening to the Jews in Europe, to his own family. His father was murdered on the street by a Nazi, his family and friends were disappearing, and he was alone far away. Out of this deep torment of terror and evil darkness descending upon the world, Neumann focused and anchored himself by studying his roots to Judaism in his new land, presenting his thoughts in his books: *The Roots of Jewish Consciousness, Volume One: Revelation and Apocalypse, Volume Two: Hasidism,* and in *Jacob and Esau.* These have only recently been published for the first time. His first book *Depth Psychology and the New Ethic* (1949) was completed during this period and published in German, but not published in English until 1969.

After the war, many children were sent to Palestine and there was an urgent need for therapists to care for them. To accommodate this need, Neumann certified child analysts. He also certified just one adult analyst: Dvora Kutzinski, who is still living and working in Tel Aviv well into her 90s, an amazingly strong, intelligent force of nature. She survived both Theresienstadt and Auschwitz.

Neumann maintained correspondence with Jung through the war with an unexplained break in communication toward the end. This is documented in their published letters, which we will discuss later. Neumann used the process of amplification to explore the archetypal patterns of expression and the symbols in myths. This work laid out for us the stadial process of development of the personality as expressed through different cultures and epochs, and how this and the biology of our common human nature reflect our own individual development. He takes us through his careful and precise understanding of the stages of conscious development in his books: *The Origins and History of Consciousness, The Great Mother, The Child, The Fear of the Feminine, Psyche and Eros, Creative Man,* and others. His first book *Depth Psychology and a New Ethic* was so challenging to the Zurich Jungians that its publication was delayed. Written during World War II, the book shared his conclusions that the historical Judeo-Christian morals and ethics were no longer useful, as seen by the evil atrocities of human behavior in the war. He argued what was needed was a new standpoint, one that shifted the ethical responsibility back to each individual, to the core and center of our being, or the greater Self. This would stop scapegoating, the cultural ritual of expelling evil.

Using the newfound ability of analysis to differentiate shadow and complex aspects of our personalities, Neumann thought we could instead develop these into what he called the ego-Self axis. Having then the functional relationship between the ego and the unconscious, we would have the ability to make our own ethical decisions based on individual human values rather than collective dogma. This book so challenged the Zurich Jungian community that they felt Neumann was trying to overstep Jung. In fact, Neumann's thesis did challenge Jung to think about *Answer to Job*[1] in a different way. Neumann was isolated from this group yet found a welcoming home at Eranos.

His writing was challenging to the reader because he introduced new concepts and descriptions as a means of clarifying and untangling the web of threads that leads us from one stage of development to another: from the original uroboros of the Great Mother or the matriarchate to the patriarchate where the masculine is present but under the control of the Great Mother, along the hero's journey to establish the ego separate from the unconscious, and finally to the patriarchy or the Great Father, where the super-ego of the outer world is established. In *The Origins and History of Consciousness,* Neumann pointed out that these are "the mythological stages in the evolution of consciousness" (1949, p. xxii). If not progressed correctly, we find ourselves or our analysands stuck at an earlier developmental stage in a neurosis where opposites are split and we are at the whims of the unconscious. Neumann takes us through the lifespan from birth to old age, assuming a successful development, reuniting once again with the unitary reality, which is where we began in the wholeness of the uroboros.

Active Imagination and Paintings

Neumann, as a young disciple of Jung's with a lifelong interest in art, learned Jung's method of active imagination as a way of bringing the images of the unconscious into reality. This enabled Neumann to move deeper into the archetypal essence and meaning of the images so they could be brought into active relationship with himself. This method is a spontaneous amplification. This important process increases consciousness, integrating shadow and complexes, which is the goal of the individuation process. After working with Jung for those six months in 1934, he took with him a huge gift in the form of this new means of engaging the psyche through word and image. I will present a series of Neumann's paintings created between mid-May 1936 and 1939. Neumann was 31 when he began the series. As we will see, he did not have the skill of a trained artist like Jung., Neumann was actually freer because of that to express himself with less precision, allowing his emotion to come through strongly. It seems that Neumann was more engaged with his personal unconscious while Jung was drawn to the archetypal realm. While both men had to explore all aspects of themselves, we know from reading Jung's early childhood dream, it was his fate or life's work to descend into the realm of the objective psyche to make sense of it for himself and for all of us. Fate befell Neumann in a different way.

Neumann had a very different life experience from Jung. As an early Zionist fascinated with the new roots growing in Palestine, he decided to leave his country of origin in 1934, all the while keenly aware of the dangers in the rise of National Socialism. He watched the horrendous atrocities befalling family members and friends, an attempt to eradicate an entire race. He was faced with pure evil and survived. In his new home, a very young Israel, he was met by a different war and new dangers, and finally the survival of his young country. It was difficult to find a safe place in the world—not just ontological danger but very real danger was everywhere. This was the *prima materia*, out of which came his book, *Depth Psychology and A New Ethic* which expressed his struggle with and understanding of evil. His focus was on his people, the Jews. Deeply considering who they were, why this would happen to them, and how to heal from this set him on his life's course.

We do not have a childhood dream from Erich Neumann to understand how his young psyche prepared him for his unique life. There are holes in our understanding of his history, both chronological and psychological, but we can glean his overall pattern of interests and struggles from his writings and paintings. We now have available the books he wrote to anchor himself in his culture and land. In Neumann's correspondence to Jung we also have record of a stunning vision: an ape-man with a single eye, representing evil, with whom Neumann struggles, finally realizing that he carries the evil within himself. We know he had this vision as he was pondering material for *Depth Psychology and The New Ethic, not the least of which was* the issue of evil, which will be discussed later.

Neumann was very interested in art and literature and the relationship between artist and culture. He wrote numerous articles on the subject, including "Art and Time," "The Creative Man and Transformation," "Leonardo da Vinci and the Mother Archetype," "Marc Chagall and the Bible," and several papers on Kafka, with whom he was fascinated. He also wrote two illustrated children's stories for his children, one on the topic of the Bible for his son and the other on the moon for his daughter. This allows us to glimpse a bit of his playful fantasy side.

We will now step into this other realm, the realm of active imagination, to witness how Erich Neumann creatively expressed his dream images in outer form through his paintings. Joining him on this journey reveals a wonderful documentation of a small piece of his process of psychological transformation, seen in the changing images.

You may be familiar with Jung's paintings in *The Red Book* and perhaps in the recently published *The Art of C. G. Jung*. In Jung's *Red Book*, we can see that Jung painted a total of 129 small and large images. Fifty-five are small, embellished letters, while 74 are half-page or full-page paintings. There are two long series: Incantations, which is twelve pages long and a series of Mandalas, eighteen pages long. Jung used repeated motifs: flowers, vines, insects, animals, and images from nature. There are many paintings that contain mosaics as backgrounds or masks. He frequently used what he called "runes" as a background, along with multicolored arabesques.

We have copies of 85 watercolors painted by Neumann. There may be more but unfortunately a portion of Neumann's writings and his active imagination paintings were sold at auction in 2006. There are 30 paintings containing women in Neumann's collection. Whereas, in Jung's *Red Book* there are only three. This is a dramatic difference considering that both worked on their relationship to the anima, their inner opposite, the feminine. Neumann has 14 paintings that contain snakes, while Jung has just five, although Jung's written active imaginations are full of conversations with his snake soul. Both men paint mosaic masks and mandalas that are quite similar. Neumann seems to have a wider range of animals in his paintings: elephants, bulls, dogs, alligators, turtles, lions, birds; and he refers to biblical and mythological figures. Jung depicted many insects and, of course, his soul in the form a snake and a dove. Jung has more imaginary figures like the death worm, cosmic dragon, Amonious, Izdubar, Atmavictu, and the gnostic and mythological figures, Phanes and Philemon.

Jung painted in gouache while Neumann chose watercolor. These are two very different mediums. The former is solid and opaque, and it can be thickly layered to cover completely. Neumann's medium was water-based and thin. The tint can be thinned with water for greater transparency or remain thicker for more intense color. Once on the paper, the effect is permanent. There is no way to rework watercolor. It is a tough and unforgiving medium. As we will see, Neumann's paintings do not need to be forgiven—they are bright, fresh and free with unapologetic mistakes. Neumann used, unblended primary colors, while Jung clearly mixed his colors and because of this he achieved greater variations in values of color, including dark and light. In a number of paintings, he used up to ten different colors. Jung also used perspective in some of his paintings while Neumann tended to leave his paintings simple and flat. We do know that Jung bought the finest paints available at the time.

Jung was meticulous. He sketched before painting, drawing in pencil on his pages in *The Red Book* before completing them with gouache. They are detailed, well planned and executed. It appears that Jung was using a different function than Neumann. Jung enlisted his sensation function in the paintings' execution, while Neumann seemed to give free reign to his emotion. Neumann, too, outlined in pencil what he would then paint. Neumann named many of his paintings, such as "The Birth" or "The Red Woman," shown in small frames on relevant pages of his journal. Like Jung, Neumann also named the prominent figures that appeared repeatedly in his art: Ashmedai, the Earth-Spirit, the Great Jew, Uranus and others. This painting series is a visual way of introducing you to Erich Neumann.

Erich Neumann's Watercolor Paintings[2]

Some paintings are dated but most are not. Neumann did not tend to date his work, and that has caused great difficulty determining not only the sequence of his paintings but certain iterations of his papers, as well. He kept journals during this period including his dreams, active imaginations and references to his paintings. At the top of some of his journal pages he sketched within a small box a likeness of the painting he discussed on that page. Some of these paintings were named but many were not. The absence of specific information makes the work of understanding these paintings like putting together a large puzzle. Thankfully, the Neumann family photographed them so we at least have copies. Erich Neumann's journals were not sold, and his daughter, Rali Neumann-Loewenthal, and Jungian analyst Tamar Kron read through them to determine the sequence of his paintings. Studying dreams and paintings in series help us see the psyche's transformational process at work. With the following paintings I will give a general archetypal amplification of the images and any known information from Neumann's dream book.

The Earth Spirit Next to the Fire.

1. This first painting is titled ***The Earth Spirit Next to the Fire***. The Earth Spirit appears more often than other figures. We know that Neumann was very interested in the Earth Spirit and the tension between Yahweh and Earth from his 1953 paper, "The Meaning of the Earth Archetype for Modern Times" (Neumann, 1994, pp. 165-226). The Earth Spirit is the figure standing next to the fire, holding what seems like flames in both hands. This would suggest that the central face with the black and brown hair is an image of Neumann's shadow, as well as an image of the Earth archetype in his unconscious. It is emerging from the central flames encompassing the instincts of nature and the underworldly creative light and heat. There is also an earth figure standing just outside of a cave with an animal like a deer. The painting consists of three distinct areas, black, blue, and green—perhaps representing the unconscious, the watery realm and the vegetative world. All three are unified by the fire. We will see these figures again and maybe have some further clarification of who they are.

The Great Jew.

2. This next painting is of ***The Great Jew***. He and Ashmedai are fighting. Ashmedai is the king of the demons, also called Asmodeus, as known from the deuterocanonical *Book of Tobit* and from the Babylonian Talmud. He is described as a monstrous creature with black wings and was instrumental to Solomon in the building of the first Temple in Jerusalem. Solomon remained terrified of this powerful demon. Could this represent the struggle Neumann had to undertake with his own dark shadow side? As discussed, he gave much thought to evil in his early book, *Depth Psychology and the New Ethic*, as well as in later papers, where he wrote "the true goal seems to be not the conquest of evil but its redemption, that one could not get rid of evil but had to attempt to transform it...a transformation of the lower worlds" (Neumann, 1994, p.195).

The Earth Spirit is Bleeding.

3. ***The Earth Spirit is Bleeding***. This is the same figure in the first slide. Again, the Earth Spirit holds what looks like fire in his left hand. He is wounded with blood dripping into a bowl while insects either drink the blood or are perhaps trying to heal him. The insects look like bees, which symbolically are connected to many gods in various myths, including

Hindu, Greek and Biblical. Their honey is a healing tincture, as well as a source of divine wisdom. They are connected to pollination, fertility, and the centrality of the matriarch. In Hebrew the word *bee* is Dvora or Deborah, who was a prophetess, the only female judge mentioned in the Bible.

The Double Egg.

4. *The Double Egg*. The journal says Ashmedai is transformed into Uranus. Uranus represents the heavens and is thought to be the son and husband of Gaia, the Earth Mother. He gave birth to the twelve Titans, three Cyclopes, and three "Hundred-Handed Ones." His son, Cronos, castrated him and became the new ruler of the universe. Astrologically, he represents originality, renewal, revolution and eccentricity. Here we see the egg containing two faces, one brown and the other grey, whereas previously the one face contained both. A differentiation is taking place in the egg, a container much like an alchemical container being heated by the flame below it. To the right is the Great Jew while on the left is Ashmedai who is said to have black wings, now Uranus with purple wings and a ladder up to the upper world. We see the three colors, black, blue, and green again with the fire in the middle acting as a connection between all three. For the first time in Neumann's artwork we see a feminine figure and an elephant on the right, the red side, and perhaps the Earth Spirit or a hero on the left with a snake above him.

Bleeding Earth Spirit, Prometheus, and the Witch.

5. *Bleeding Earth Spirit, Prometheus, and the Witch*. Prometheus is the small figure on the mountain in the middle climbing up to steal fire. The fire is needed to bring the life energy from the gods to the human realm. This task is that of the hero that is us all, to separate from the Great Mother, the matriarchal uroboros, and later from the remaining aspects of the cloying maternal witch trying to hold us firmly in her grasp. We always encounter this aspect of the psyche first, that shadow aspect of the great feminine, who is both the Good and Terrible Mother, our primary archetype. Here she seems to take the fire for cooking. Fire represents consciousness, light, heat, warmth and the beginning of human civilization.

Three Stairs.

6. *Three Stairs*. Here again is Uranus changed from Ashmedai, the transformer who moves from one realm to another, up and down the ladder as angel, demon, trickster. He brings fire in one hand and what looks like a snake in the other. He has become the bridge between the heavens and the earth, where both sides of this archetype are now conscious. Three represents relationship and a coming into consciousness, but not yet whole.

The World Wheel.

7. This painting is called ***The World Wheel***. Something is growing, emerging from the center of the human figure that stands within the world wheel. The wheel is a mandala surrounding a human at its center, referring to humans as being the central fulcrum of the movement of the world with all opposites revolving around us. Only we and our increased consciousness are able to create psychic wholeness.

8. ***Uranus Spreads Himself Out***. The whole scene seems to be in an egg. Again, we have those two faces, blond and grey, which are now separate, with Uranus in between standing on something like an egg incubating the Red One, a feminine figure, the anima. Fire, water, earth and something white flow into her as she lies between the earth forces and the fire from the gods. The fire is now in the earthly realm, perhaps here used as an offering to the spirit realm.

Uranus Spreads Himself Out.

The Red.

9. *The Red*. She emerged out of the prior egg and is clearly something like the feminine embodiment of the earth. These two other figures appear in other paintings and they have a potent connection to the earthly realm. In his letters to Jung, Neumann writes in 1934 about the first appearance of his anima:

> As you prophesied, the anima has gone to ground. She made an appearance all nice and brown, strikingly Africa, even more impenetrable in me, domineering—with a sisterly relationship to many animals—a boa constrictor, a panther, an elephant, a wild horse and a rhinoceros—thus speaks an image. (Jung-Neumann, 2015, 5N, p. 16)

The anima is the mediator between us and others, the Thou of the *I-Thou* relationship. It mediates between earth and heaven, sustaining the ego-Self axis. This figure brings with it emotions, perhaps desire, fear, joy, aliveness, creativity, playfulness for him to get to know in himself. Stepping into the world of affect, instincts and chaos requires a step away from the patriarchy and its prevailing cultural values of rationality, dogma and obedience. The Earth archetype is the Dark Mother, both Good and Terrible, life giving and taking.

The Blessing.

10. ***The Blessing***. The Red one is being blessed from above and from below through the snake, the transformer Mercurius that brings riches from the creative depths with a flow of energy reaching all three realms.

The Blossoming Earth Spirit.

11. ***The Blossoming Earth Spirit***. Life is growing in this beautiful serene watercolor of flowers and plants blossoming. This is such an important alchemical moment.

The Rising Earth Spirit.

12. ***The Rising Earth Spirit***. Something is in the transformation process, incubating symbolically out of the stars in the center, as if a mandala is forming, releasing its life energy.

The Pregnant Woman.

13. ***The Pregnant Woman***. This is the next natural step in this individuation process. First the trickster steals fire from the gods, then the spark is transferred to the world. Nature herself is born and fertilized out of the potent symbol and union of above and below. It lands within the womb of the human as she seems to stand between the greyish spirit on the right—perhaps the union of the black haired and brown and blond haired faces, and the demon himself in the branches of a tree, who has a mosaic-like face with horns. The woman now holds the fire, perhaps the same life energy that was released from the mandala in the last painting. As is true for all humans, we stand between the opposing realms of nature and spirit. We are the ones who have to navigate that middle ground.

14. ***Birth***. Here we now have the birth of the child, protected by the opposing forces from the prior painting, now engaged and helpful. The child is the symbol of new life. Each spirit seems to bring a gift—grapes and a flame, like Dionysus and Apollo both present.

Birth.

The Diamond Flower Inside the Wheel.

15. *The Diamond Flower Inside the Wheel*. Now the process moves to the symbolic realm and is a symbol of the Self, in this beautiful naturalistic mandala. From the earth emerges the mandala, showing the union that has been formed in Neumann's psyche through his process of individuation as seen in these images. It was his desire to find his Jewish roots in his new land, grounded in nature.

The One Who Sits on the Throne.

16. ***The One Who Sits on the Throne***. The child has been enthroned on what appears to be a primordial earthly realm filled with trees, animals, water, earth, and the passionately bright, yellow sun-filled sky. The child's arms are lifted in celebration or gratitude for the birth of this realm. The snake encircles the divine child's container. The red cow at the bottom of the mountain appears in other paintings. As much of a story as it is, we are invited into Neumann's myth, a small but significant part of his individuation process. One wants to rest here a while with the incredible story of his psychic struggle to find wholeness, but this is not possible for very long.

The Pain of the World.

17. ***The Pain of the World***. The reality of the shadow side is ever present; we cannot and should not forget it. The year is 1938. This painting was painted on March 12th. Eight months later, the nightmare of Chrystal Night befell Germany and the Jews, a reminder of the very real existence of evil. From Israel, Neumann knew what was taking place in Germany. The three figures and animals seem stuck in the blackness of the unconscious, as if nature and consciousness were being repressed downward in an untenable cave. A fire, not connected to the surface, is locked away with them. The Jewish souls go up in flames. The wild strokes of blue emanate from the black pyramid along with the red lightening and flames from above. Could this be the evil side of the Self let loose in the collective unconscious of the Germans? The green of nature is suppressed. It strikes me that unhinged intuitive thinking represented by the color blue has been unleashed along with destructive passion and emotion in red—a dangerous combination.

The World Hour.

18. ***The World Hour***. This is the last of the series, as far as we know. This was painted between April 18th and April 28th of the same year. The psyche, true to form, thankfully compensates for the horror of the prior painting. The process cycles up and down, from one side to the other, positive to negative, just as the ocean tides come in and recede in a never-ending cycle. We shift to the archetypal realm with this painting, far away from the reality of evil in the world. Here we find hope and balance in the three realms including sun, moon and a beautiful arch, appearing to be the cycle of life and time that contains all. But we cannot forget the presence of the snake in the red and black encasement at the bottom of the scene. Evil exists and Neumann never forgot that. His life work was to make sense of evil and understand consciousness. The mosaic-faced demon is not really a devil but more a nature spirit. There are opposites but not really in conflict. What seems of importance is finding balance. The truth that emerges is that the only horror is man-made.

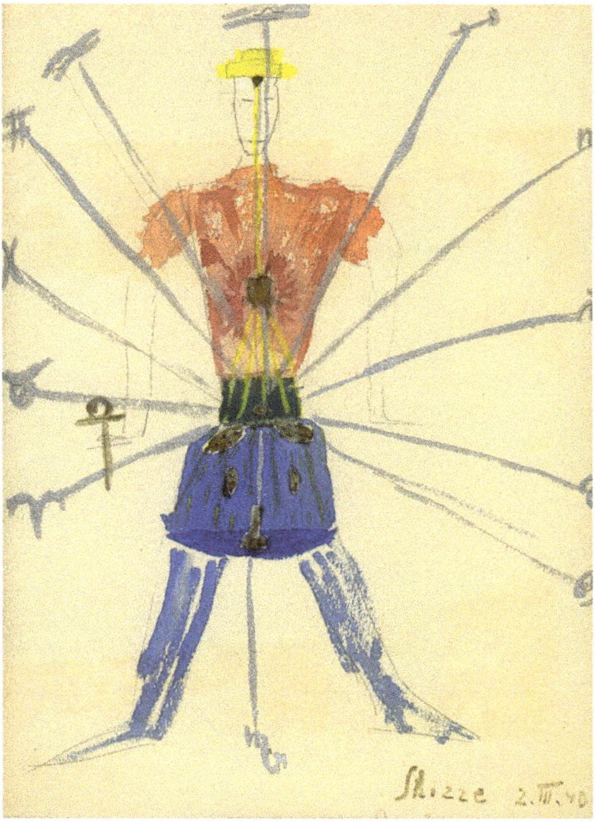

Astrological Signs.

19. *Astrological Signs*. This painting was painted in 1940, later than the rest. It is of a figure Neumann paints frequently, the Anthropos. Here he is surrounded by the zodiac pointing to fate given to each one of us and our relation to the cosmos. But of course, we influence our fate through the choices we make, creating our own destinies. In 1949, Neumann writes in his paper, "Mystical Man:"

> The image of the Anthropos surrounded by circles of heavens and hells, which originate within him, resembles the mandala of ancient astrology. But once the phenomenon of projection has been understood, this conception of man's position in the cosmos gives way to one far more complicated, one which loses

> in clarity what it gains in dynamism.... The world is the carrier of the projections of the unconscious, and with the development of the human ego, which takes back and makes conscious these projections, our image both of the cosmos and of man changes....The personality is continuously being changed from its own center outward by the spontaneous action of the creative unconscious. (1961, p. 10-11)

Neumann reveals in his writing that his ascendant in his astrological chart is Leo at 0°, while his sun sign is at 2° Aquarius and his moon sign is 4° Virgo, for those of you who understand astrology.

Concluding Thoughts

To understand Neumann's place in analytical psychology, it is helpful to place him next to Jung, as much of his work was stimulated through their interactions; though Neumann, an independent thinker, always had his own strong viewpoints. Neumann began analysis with Jung at 28, three years after Jung stopped working on *The Red Book* and shifted his attention to alchemy. Neumann was 31 years old when he undertook his own journey into the depths. While there was a 31 year age difference between the two men, Jung died seven months after Neumann, who tragically died of kidney cancer at the age of 55. Although we have more information about Jung's journey, Neumann's is equally valuable for the clarity of his process provided by his paintings. This work offers the viewer a clearer experience of Erich Neumann and how he works with the psyche. Frequently images are clearer than words. They bring with them a mix of rational, archetypal, personal and transpersonal, filled with evocative emotion. As we know from the images in our dreams, we cannot hide from the full experience presented to us by images.

ENDNOTES

[1] Jung, C. G. (1958). Answer to Job, in *CW11*, pp. 365-470. Princeton: Princeton University Press.

[2] Nineteen of Erich Neumann's watercolor paintings © Erich Neumann, Courtesy of the Erich Neumann Estate.

CHAPTER II

Analysis of The Jung-Neumann Correspondence

From their correspondence, Jung described Neumann as one of his closest friends with whom he could share his forming thoughts, accept criticism, criticize back, and remain always respectful and enthusiastic. These two brilliant men, sharing a substantial age difference, challenged each other, supported each other, and did not mince words with each other—ever. It is accurately described as a creative relationship, one that deepened and widened the thoughts and understandings of both men. We are the beneficiaries of this interaction which lasted until the end of their lives.

Reading their correspondence, one is struck by the intimacy and genuine caring between the two men. Neumann, the young man, learned from Jung and one sees his development and deepening of understanding over the years. Jung was patient, supportive and honest while at the same time challenged to look at his responses to the rise of National Socialism and learn more about Judaism.

I would like to begin by quoting from the letters to give you a sense of the friendship we are dealing with. These quotes are from later in their lives, when two old men soften and risks are no longer a concern. Neumann's early death from kidney cancer was tragic. He did not live long enough to shepherd his many creative endeavors properly into the world, and we do not have the benefit of the works he could have undertaken had he lived. His previously unpublished manuscripts *Jacob and Esau: On the Collective Symbolism of the Brother Motif, and The Roots of Jewish Consciousness, Volume One & Two* have now been published, including his brilliant, unfinished book *The Child* (1990b), which was published posthumously.

Neumann ran into constant sibling rivalry in the Jungian world. From these quotes you can guess why. Jung to Neumann in 1955:

> I would like to sincerely thank you not only that you have taken to the pen for me in such a generous way, but also for that greater thing that you are achieving in your life's work....Men like you are rare birds whose perspective the world needs. (Jung & Neumann, 2015, p. 310, letter 103J)

Neumann to Jung in 1955: "I constantly consider this interweaving with your work as one of the finest gifts of my life. And I know that even where you see accents differently from the way I do that I am someone who, in your eyes, is taking it forward" (Neumann, 2015, p. 313, letter 104N).

Further in 1958, Neumann told Jung:

> My link with you is, as you know, not dependent on writing and speaking, nor no longer dependent, I should say, but meeting with you always brings me a substantial affirmation that cannot be found anywhere else in the world. I hope you understand what I mean. For me, there is only you yourself as a 'connecting point' in the center, as far as the task of the work is concerned. (2015, p. 342, letter 117N)

And finally, Jung to Julia Neumann on her husband's death in 1961: "I was particularly shattered by the unexpected and, for me, sudden death of my friend and companion on the way in whose fate I participated in tranquility and from a distance" (2015, p. 354, letter 121J).

Essential conflict

Interestingly, Jung had visited Palestine in 1933 and found it quite chaotic, perhaps recognizing how difficult it would be for the Jews to carve out their independent state in that land. Jung writes to Neumann in 1938:

> I am right in the thick of it and am following the Palestinian question on a daily basis in the newspapers, and think often of my acquaintances there who have to live in this chaos. When I was in Palestine in 1933, I was unfortunately able to see what was coming all too clearly. I also foresaw great misfortune for Germany, even quite terrible things, but when it then shows up, it still seems unbelievable (Jung & Neumann, 2015, p. 145, letter 28J).

This letter arrived in December 1938, and Jung did not specifically mention the horror of Kristallnacht.

By 1934, towards the end of his stay in Zurich, Neumann sent a letter to Jung that began with his strong criticism of what Jung wrote in his 1934 paper, "The State of Psychotherapy Today" (Jung, 1978, pp. 157-173, par. 333-370). This paper is a criticism of Freud's approach to therapy and reveals how Jung and his Germanic psyche may have been misunderstood. Jung, in contrast to Freud, emphasizes the importance of recognizing the subtle, unique differences between people and criticizes Freud for reducing patients to an infantile "nothing but," and falling back on the use of technique as opposed to being "absolutely clear in his own mind that psychological treatment of the sick is a relationship in which the doctor is involved quite as much as the patient" (Jung, 1978, p. 146, par. 352). Jung maintained that in all neuroses there exist positive elements that shed light on the health of the individual, as well as what is commonly seen as negative. In his paper, Jung sternly criticized Freud and his reductionist technique:

> Psychoanalysis is evidently a technique behind which the human being vanishes, and which always remains the same no matter who practices it. Consequently, the psychoanalyst needs no self-knowledge and no criticism of his assumptions. Apparently the purpose of this training analysis is to make him not a human being but a correct applier of technique. (Jung, 1978, p. 163)

As his antipathy builds he suddenly shifted from discussing Freud to speaking in broad, general terms about Jews, comparing them to women who are physically weaker, "they have to aim at the chinks in the armour of their adversary, and thanks to this technique which has been forced on them through the centuries, the Jews themselves are best protected where others are most vulnerable" (Jung, 1978, p. 165). Is it possible that Jung slipped into a complex here resulting from a wound left over from his relationship with Freud? Did he feel Freud was "protected" while he, Jung, was "vulnerable?" He then continued to discuss the differences between Jews and Germanic peoples. This is where it became offensive to Neumann. Jung referred to the emergent movement out of the Germanic/ Slavic psyche as having two sides: one that is pathological and the other that is potentially creative, "laboring at the future" (Jung, 1978, p. 161, par, 354). It is clear that Jung was quite taken with the potential he saw in the Germanic psyche as he described its capacity to create new cultural forms, "seeds bursting with energy and capable of mighty expansion" (1978, p. 165, par. 353). This line of thinking paralleled his earlier statements on individuals' neuroses containing both negative and positive seeds, yet with his shift to speaking broadly about cultural groups he seemed to have lost his subtle discernment. Jung asserted that the Germanic psyche carries the greatest, youthful potential while Jews as a group carry their shadow between the conscious and unconscious because of their older culture. While Jung reduced Jews to the assimilated European culture Jew he was familiar with, like Freud, he warned against using "Jewish categories" on Germanic-Slavic Christendom because, "their creative and intuitive depth of soul—has been explained as a morass of banal infantilism, while my own warning voice has for decades been suspected of anti-Semitism. This suspicion emanated from Freud" (1978, p. 166). One can clearly feel the animosity emanating from his writing. Is it Freud or Jews Jung criticizes or are they both mixed together, which Neumann suspects?

Of course, Neumann would respond to this line of thinking with great disappointment and dismay, not understanding why this great man was overgeneralizing in an incorrect way and seemingly did not see what he and many others saw so clearly, "that it is also in the Germanic psyche (and in the Slavic one) that a mind-numbing cloud of filth, blood and rottenness is brewing" (Jung & Neumann, 2015, p. 12, letter 4N). Could it be that Jung's own complex blinded him? When one is caught in a complex one overgeneralizes, loses one's grounded balance, and gets caught by one side of an archetype.

With the rise of National Socialism out of the Germanic/Slavic psyche Jung saw a germ of an unknown potential catch fire. Steeped in his own feelings around Freudian psychology and having experienced himself as misunderstood, one might see how he came to give value to the new emerging spark out of the Germanic/Slavic psyche. Neumann took issue with how Jung too broadly equated National Socialism with the Aryan-Germanic, and how he misunderstood and generalized Jews. Jung said, "The Jew, who is something of a nomad, has never yet created a cultural form of his own and as far as we can see never will, since all his instincts and talents require a more or less civilized nation to act as host for their development" (Jung, 1978, pp. 165-167, par. 353). Neumann took offence at Jung leaning here towards a "race-psychology," believing that all Jews should not be put into the same box lacking any depth of exploration into Jewish culture, past and present. He speaks of the differences between religious and assimilated Jews, and the development of Zionism and Hasidism, making clear: This Jewish renaissance seems to me to be more embryonic, youthful and full of energy than the Nazi-rigid, brutally organized and stolid, extreme submissiveness of the Aryan revivals (Jung & Neumann, 2015, p. 14, letter 4N).

It is striking how strong this young man was in his convictions and thinking. He caught Jung in a blind spot and challenged him on it. One wonders why Jung did not speak up about his misstatements and deeds at this point. We know Jung was later blacklisted by Adolf Hitler. During the war, Jung worked for Allen Dulles of the OSS, now the CIA, as agent 488 helping to explain the psychology of Hitler. We don't know why communication stopped between Jung and Neumann between 1940 and 1945. In his paper, "After the Catastrophe" (Jung, 1970, Vol. 10) Jung stated:

> Clearly these misgivings came much too late; but even so, it is just conceivable that Hitler himself may have had good intentions at first, and only succumbed to the use of the wrong means, or the misuse of his means, in the course of his development....But I should like to emphasize above all that it is part and parcel of the pathological liar's make-up to be plausible. Therefore it is no easy matter, even for experienced people, to form an opinion, particularly while the plan is still apparently in the idealistic stage. It is then quite impossible to foresee how things are likely to develop and Mr. Chamberlain's "give-it-a-chance" attitude seems to be the only policy. (1970, p. 206, par. 421)

Jung had described Hitler as inhuman, and must have known that his way was to deceive. Could Jung have been so easily deceived? Did he fall into his own blind spot? Was he too identified with the hopefulness of the Aryan-Germanic psyche, being Germanic himself? Was he blinded by something with the potential for evil? Evil, the subject of "the finest and deepest of your books," as Neumann described *Answer to Job*, was a clear preoccupation of Jung as well, and frequent subject in their correspondence (Jung & Neumann, 2015, p. 271, 86N). This seems to point to Jung's need to understand the depths of this universal quandary. Gershom Scholem writes in a letter to Aniela Jaffé in 1963 that Jung acknowledged to Leo Baeck: "Well, I slipped up." Jaffé concluded from this: "probably referring to the Nazis and his expectation that something great might after all emerge" (1989, p. 100).

So, what then was Jung's blind spot? Was it that he was fascinated by the potential creative contents that can emerge out of the collective unconscious and, therefore, expressed his thoughts in broad sweeping generalized ways? At times, Neumann as well tended to sweeping generalizations, such as: "One must not forget that the Christian peoples have never deemed the Jews worthy of their conscious interest" (Jung & Neumann, 2015, p. 45, letter 6N). At other times, both Jung and Neumann focused on the importance of individual anomalies and propensities, clearly emphasizing the individual experience. What I found stunning in the correspondence, though, was how frequently Jung seemed to remain neutral, standing back and watching the opposite sides of an archetype or conflict play out as they would, rather than forming an opinion on one side or the other.

Jung's comments on Jewish character and Judaism point to a man who seemed in the early 1930s to be either naïve or lacking understanding. Neumann recognized this and took him to task for not studying Judaism as he did so many other religions and cultures.

Jung was a thinker who struggled with his feeling function, as we can see in the *Red Book* with his difficult journey into the Spirit of the Depths to find his soul, and in relation to those around him. As he says of himself late in life in *Memories, Dreams, Reflections* (1989):

> I have offended many people, for as soon as I saw that they did not understand me that was the end of the matter as far as I was concerned. I had to move on. I had no patience with people—aside from my patients. I had to obey an inner law which was imposed on me and left me no freedom of choice….I had to learn painfully that people continued to exist even when they had nothing more to say to me. (pp. 356-357)

He may have been more interested in the broader archetypal stirrings in German culture than its effect on individual human beings. I can understand this interest; while appalled, I am fascinated by the shifting archetypal patterns that produced ISIS, the Taliban, and Vladimir Putin's invasion of Ukraine, at times overlooking the devastating consequences upon individuals caught in the crossfire. Perhaps we would like to hold Jung to a higher standard than we hold ourselves. But just like everyone on this path, he had to struggle with his humanity, his opposites, and his own process of individuation.

Jewish Psychology

In 1937 when in Zurich, Neumann described experiencing a "rush" of images that left him, "now convinced of the authenticity of the phenomena" (Jung & Neumann, 2015, p. 131, letter 24N). It seems the reality of the psyche, as the earth spirit and transformed anima, broke through his rational mind, which seems to be confirmed by the images he describes in his dreams and visions around that time.

Two other important issues discussed in the correspondence are Jewish psychology, and evil. Neumann encouraged Jung to study Judaism, specifically the Hasidic movement and Kabbalah. The focus of Neumann's early years was on this topic and out of it emerged the vision for a book with three or perhaps four parts, *The Roots of Jewish Consciousness* or *On the Depth Psychology of the Modern Jew*. Part one is *The Problem of Revelation in Jewish Antiquity*. Part two is *The Psychological Meaning of Hasidism*, and the third is *Religious Experience in Depth Analysis*. The first part studies the Jewish historical preconditions while the second studies the development of Hasidism as the bridge between the God-principle and the earth-principle, including a deeper understanding of the Shekinah.

Neumann first framed his discussion of the development of Jewish psychology on the Biblical story of Jacob and Esau, the warring brothers, in which Jacob steals the birthright from Esau and therefore is entitled to his father's blessing. Neumann described Jacob as being introverted and of the nature of the moon, while Esau was extraverted and of the sun. The moon-like nature is interior-focused and worships YHWH while the sun nature is outer-focused on the material world and connected to the hairy goat or the devil. The two reconcile in the end, and, as Neumann argued, this reflects the process of individuation, bringing the opposites together and integrating the shadow. Neumann's thinking on this topic, which developed in dialogue in his letters with Jung, crystallized into Neumann's first book–though only recently published.

Jung did take up the study of this material as is evident by the books of Kabbalah in his library. According to a letter from Aniela Jaffé to Rivkah Schärf, he thanked her for the texts, though this was not mentioned in his letters to Neumann (2015, p.29). Nevertheless, in 1944 Jung had an important vision which places him in the garden of the pomegranates with the union of the male and female principles within the Godhead. This makes it clear what an impact the Jewish tradition and the Kabbalah had on his psyche! Jung wrote in *Memories Dreams and Reflections* (1989):

> For a time it seemed to me that she [the nurse] was an old Jewish woman, much older than she actually was, and that she was preparing ritual kosher dishes for me. When I looked at her, she seemed to have a blue halo around her head. I myself was, so it seemed, in the Pardes Rimmonim, the garden of pomegranates, and the wedding of Tifereth with Malchuth was taking place. Or else I was Rabbi Simon ben Jochai [who wrote the Zohar], whose wedding in the afterlife was being celebrated. It was the mystic marriage as it appears in Cabbalistic tradition. I cannot tell you how wonderful it was.... At bottom it was I myself: I was the marriage. And my beatitude was that of a blissful wedding. (p. 294)

In letter 29 N, November 15, 1939, Neumann wrote Jung of a dream he had that refers to the work of the *pardes.*[1] Neumann's discussion in this letter is on his struggle with the central Jewish problem of intuition that is linked to a rootlessness of the Jewish structure. He acknowledges that the symbolism of the Jew is consistent with the European, though it "would have been simpler if a specific symbolism could have been demonstrated." He saw something secular transpiring, pertaining to the individual as "revelation-center and realization-center of the Self." As he said, his "attempt to create the continuity through to the modern Jewish person from the openness to revelation of antiquity via the inner Hasidic revolution is, as I well know myself, a new interpretation" (Jung & Neumann, 2015 p. 149, letter 29N). His work, then, came to "circle [s] around the YHWH earth opposite" (2015, p.151-152).
This reveals the Hasidic influence on his thinking and his intuition of a new interpretation. He wrote:

> In Hasidism, the last breakthrough of actual introverted Judaism, all these problems broadly came of age. The redemption of the

> "sparks" out of matter, for example, is, put psychologically, arguably the taking back of the world into internal space. In this way, everything, every action, every fulfillment of the law can lead to "higher union," to the encounter with YHWH, and so the structure of the world can be experienced as one that is at the same time "unified" and that is full of YHWH. (2015, p. 42, letter 6N (A))

Neumann, in the same letter continued, "YHWH is constantly changing his manifestation, but at the same time he is always the same" (p. 42). And further,

> For me YHWH is not an archetype, but the 'God' archetype is only an interchangeable theophany of YHWH about which there is nothing more to be said, other than how he appears and what form his "so-called energetic structure" takes, being superior to the appearance itself. (2015, p.49, letter 6N (A))

Angelica Loewe described Neumann's perception of the Jewish exegesis as, "an introduction and initiation into the revelation of eternity in the midst of time" (as revelation is continuing, including in the present) and compares it to the Christian exegesis which aims at, "progress through time towards eternity" (where revelation comes at the end of time).[2]

This reflects the differences in viewpoints between Judaism and Christianity—but not between Neumann and Jung. Both focused on real time transformation taking place within the individual. One can gather from Neumann's discussion that God for him was very real and beyond the laws of the archetypes. God changes manifestations or takes on different archetypal faces but is not identified with any one. It is similar to Brahma in Hindu theology, a conglomeration of gods making up the one.

For Jung, God in itself was unknowable and beyond the opposites. Psychologically, though, it can be described as the archetype of wholeness, the Self, containing all opposites Humans perceive the manifestation of the archetype of wholeness as the "God-image." This image takes on different cultural forms. Since the archetype of wholeness contains everything, is there something beyond this? It seems both Jung and Neumann would say yes.

After writing the above monographs on Jewish psychology, Neumann's interests refocused on psychology in general. This may have had to do with the fact that the need in Israel after the war was acute with the arrival of Holocaust survivors and traumatized children who needed real time care.

After the War

As mentioned, from 1940 to 1945 there was no correspondence between Erich Neumann and Jung. Nevertheless, Neumann remained acutely aware of what was taking place in Europe, and he remained very busy with his increasing practice and his writing. Following the years of war in Europe, times were uncertain in Israel. The British mandate came to an end, and there was great uncertainty in 1948 whether the newly formed state would survive the attacks from neighboring countries. In fact, the house next door to the Neumann's was bombed, during which one child died and eighteen were wounded.[3] In 1945 Neumann had sent Jung his manuscript, *Depth Psychology and the New Ethic,* which renewed their conversations. It is interesting that they did not talk about what went on in Europe during the war years. One can only speculate that his sending Jung his book was a way of expressing his thoughts on the horror that took place, without falling into the devastating feeling of it. Both men were thinking types, and inferior feeling gets very messy. It is, nonetheless, present in a very deep way, just difficult to articulate.

Jung's last comments to Neumann in 1940 before their lapse of communication for five years included, "As you know, we live here in Switzerland on an island with reduced heating. Otherwise there is nothing new to report" (Jung & Neumann, 2015, p. 158, letter 32J). There had been no mention of Kristallnacht in 1938, this was as evocative as he got. Then in 1945 when they resumed communication Neumann stated, "I am writing nothing about the times, nothing about Palestine. My inner dialectic indicated the only possible path for me. At these times, the general human condition moves me and this only. How else could one bear it" (p. 163, letter 33N). Jung added in his first letter, "While we are still living on our cultural island as before, everything around us is nothing but destruction, physically as well as morally. To do something reasonable oneself, you have to close your eyes. Germany is indescribably rotten" (2015, p. 171, letter 37J).

We know the horrors of this war and the destruction that it left in its wake and can only imagine its impact on the individual psyche. Jung is frequently criticized for not discussing his experience during the war in his correspondence with Neumann. In fact, Jung's work as secret agent number 488 and front man in Europe tasked with giving OSS Director Allen Dulles psychological insights into Hitler's personality and potential behaviors likely explains this. Dulles later remarked, "Nobody will probably ever know how much Prof. Jung contributed to the allied cause during the war" (Mark Vernon, 2011). In 1945, Jung wrote "After the Catastrophe" in which he offered his thoughts on the madness that overtook Germany during WWII. Although not expressed in a letter to Neumann, it is clear that Jung felt and thought deeply about what had transpired. Jung wrote:

> Long before 1933 there was a smell of burning in the air, and people were passionately interested in discovering the locus of the fire and in tracking down the incendiary. And when denser clouds of smoke were seen to gather over Germany, and the burning of the Reichstag gave the signal, then at last there was no mistake where the incendiary, evil in person, dwelt... The sight of evil kindles evil in the soul....Something of the abysmal darkness of the world has broken in on us, poisoning the very air we breathe and befouling the pure water with the stale, nauseating taste of blood. (Jung, 1970, p. 199)

Jung continued:

> When evil breaks at any point into the order of things, our whole circle of psychic protection is disrupted....The phenomenon we

> have witnessed in Germany was nothing less than the first outbreak of epidemic insanity, an eruption of the unconscious into what seemed to be a tolerably well-ordered world. A whole nation, as well as countless millions belonging to other nations, were swept into the blood-drenched madness of a war of extermination. (Jung, p. 200) Hitler was the exponent of a "new order," and that is the real reason why practically every German fell for him. ... like the rest of the world, they did not understand wherein Hitler's significance lay, that he symbolized something in every individual. He was the most prodigious personification of all human inferiorities. ... He represented the shadow, the inferior part of everybody's personality, in an overwhelming degree, and this was another reason why they fell for him. In Hitler, every German should have seen his own shadow, his own worst danger. (Jung, p. 223)

Conflict in Zurich and Discussion of Evil

One can only imagine how difficult it would have been to move beyond what had recently transpired in Europe. The world was changed forever; and the friendship between Jung and Neumann resumed. I begin this next section with a quote from Jung. "I would like to avoid the emergence of some sort of orthodoxy that pushes out other types of individuality" (Jung & Neumann, 2015, 247, 75J). In 1948 Neumann presented a paper at Eranos and at the newly formed Jung Institute on *The New Ethic* (published in German in 1949), which created a huge stir. It was rejected, vilified, treated as an apostasy, thought to be anti-Christian, and to deviate too far from Jung. Jung, of course, saw this coming and actually said to Neumann beforehand after reading it, "I cannot conceal from you my secret pleasure...your writings will be a *petra scandali*, but also the powerful impetus for future developments. For this I am most deeply grateful to you" (p. 237, letter 72J).

Many in the Jungian world were more interested in following Jung, sticking to their own perceived guidelines of what Jungian psychology was all about. Not Neumann, an original thinker appreciated greatly by Jung.

Thus, particularly Neumann's lectures evoked strong criticisms by Jolanda Jacobi, C. A. Meier, and Toni Wolff.

The C.G. Jung Institute in Kusnacht was established in 1948 with Jung as its nominal president and C. A. Meier as vice-president. Neumann's hope to publish *The Origins and History of Consciousness*, initially selected to be the first Institute publication, was subsequently rejected by Meier. He and others felt it would dwarf any books that followed. There was a myriad of criticism about it, especially that Neumann too neatly formed a system, as if contrary to Jung's theory. The dislike of *The New Ethic* didn't help this situation. Instead of Neumann's book being published first, Meier published his own much smaller book, *Healing Dream and Ritual: Ancient Incubation and Modern Psychotherapy.*

Supportive of Neumann's writings, Jung stood up for Neumann and helped him get it published instead by Rascher Verlag in German and Kegan Paul in English. What is apparent is that there was a strong sense of sibling rivalry from the Zurich Jungians against Neumann, and he was effectively ostracized from participating there for many years, although he also chose to avoid such a disagreeable environment. As an extremely introverted man, he kept to himself much of the time except for his very active practice. He found himself quite alone in Tel Aviv.

Neumann's communications and periodic visits to Zurich to work with Jung were a lifeline for him. Overall there were sixty-two letters from Neumann to Jung, forty-six from Jung to Neumann. From 1947 on, at the initial recommendation of Jung, Eranos became a supportive intellectual *temenos* for Neumann. His first paper was "Mystical Man," presented in 1948. Because of his well-received participation there, Olga Froebe-Kapteyn, the founder of Eranos, requested that Neumann write up a monograph using the picture archive she created.[4] This grew into a book, *The Great Mother,* and additional papers that formed the foundation for his other books. Eranos provided Neumann with the broad intellectual environment that he found most satisfying.

Neumann, the ever sensitive one, did not feel that Jung defended him sufficiently against the criticism. In a later letter to Olga Froebe-Kapteyn on May 22, 1949 he understood this as a manifestation of the broad sweep of anti-Semitism that infected Europe at that time. In fact, the Jung Institute in Zurich did have a rule on the books limiting the number of Jewish members until it was revoked in early 1950 after Sigmund Hurwitz refused to join because of it. Much later, Jerome Bernstein asked then president Alfred Ribi to apologize for this. Initially angry and resistant, Ribi acquiesced in the end.[5]

When Neumann was once again criticized at his lecture on *Amor and Psyche*, Jung, upon hearing about it, gave a group of colleagues from the Institute a solid lashing down:

> One should not have discussed the problems in public. It is so finely nuanced that it is not possible to sort it out in a discussion. But above all, one can't load these things onto N. in public. .... Besides, one must not forget that he has been in Palestine on his own for nine years. When he worked with me back then, many things which you are learning today had not even been uttered. When he left, we did not yet know much that we know today. And besides, we are not dealing with a theory, but a human being. You cannot do this right in the middle of a course. I would like to see the animus in you if you were to be corrected in a lecture. If I had been there, I would have attempted to rectify some things. But I would have said it only once and then shut up. N. is very sensitive, easily gets upset. But he is a creative man. And one should not upset such people. Leave him alone. (2015, p. 288, note 518)

One can see how their relationship was challenging to both men but the final sensibility is expressed unequivocally by Jung when he is reported to have said, "I have a huge correspondence, see innumerable people but have only two real friends with whom I can speak about my own difficulties; the one is Erich Neumann and he lives in Israel and the other is Father Victor White in England" (Jung & White, 2007, p. 334).

The New Ethic certainly challenged many established notions of the time, and before Jung agreed to write the foreword to the book he gave

Neumann a list of points to consider as supplementary suggestions. Jung's position was different from Neumann's, who points out that this has to do with the fact that Jung is an Occidental Christian while Neumann, a Jew, is more of the East.

Even though Neumann's book, *The New Ethic,* ran into severe criticism in Zurich, Jung thought Neumann's thinking was brilliant, and modified or deleted a portion of his paper "A Psychological View of Conscience,"[6] as a result of Neumann's responses to Jung's criticism of his book.

While agreeing with most of *The New Ethic,* Jung began his discussion of the book by stating that there is a difference in language. He pointed out that there is no new ethic, what Neumann is proposing is the same old ethic, more differentiated and with fewer illusions (Jung & Neumann, 2015, p. 329, 112J). Jung ended by saying he is unsure what is right as he does not have a clear answer and will have to leave the dilemma to God himself. His position was that evil will befall us and there is really nothing we can do as it is unconscious. He said:

> Evil is and always remains the thing one knows one should not do. Man overestimates himself unfortunately in this respect: he thinks it is within his discretion to intend good or evil. He can persuade himself of this, but in reality he is, in view of the greatness of these opposites, simply too small and too unconscious to be able to choose the one or the other in free will and under all circumstances. It is much more the case that he does or does not do the good that he would like to for overwhelming reasons, and that in the same way, evil just happens to him like misfortune.
>
> Ethics is that which makes it impossible for him to do evil intentionally and encourages him to do good—and indeed often with little success. I.e., he can do good and cannot avoid evil, although his ethic causes him to test the powers of his will in this regard. In reality he is the victim of these powers...under no circumstances can he absolutely avoid sin, as he also on the other hand may hope to be able to do good. Now, as evil is

> unavoidable, so one never completely evades sin and it is a fact that one must accept. (pp. 327-328, 112J)

Jung framed this in an ethical light: since we cannot avoid sin, how can we deal with this situation? From a Christian standpoint, one accepts the fact of sin and lives with it, trying to be as good as possible for the Lord and also morally substantial to appear good to others. Earlier in his list of suggested revisions Jung emphasized, "that the shadow or the unconscious absolutely cannot be eliminated and subject to consciousness. We can only learn how a grain of corn must behave between a hammer and anvil" (Jung, 2015, p. 361, Appendix II). This is actually quite a pessimistic point of view.

Neumann received this criticism and responded strongly with impressive conviction. For him, he said: "*The New Ethic* was the attempt to process a series of phantasies that roughly corresponded time-wise with the extermination of the Jews, and in which the problem of evil and justice was being tossed around in me" (Jung & Neumann, 2015, 113N, p. 331). Then he had a profound vision after which the world looked different:

> I seemed to be commissioned to kill the apeman in the profound primal hole. As I approached him, he was hanging, by night, sleeping on the cross above the abyss, but his—crooked—single eye was staring into the depths of this abyss. While it at first seemed that I was supposed to blind him, I all of a sudden grasped his 'innocence,' his dependence on the single eye of the godhead, which was experiencing the depths through him, which was a human eye. Then, very abridged, I sank down opposite this single eye, jumped into the abyss, but was caught by the Godhead, which carried me on the 'wings of his heart.' After that, this single eye opposite the apeman closed and it opened on my forehead. (Bit difficult to write this, but what should one do). (2015, p. 331)

Neumann discussed evil in relation to his psyche's clarification in the dream as being something he had to experience, it was not sin but a necessary action. In his vision, he jumped into the abyss, rather than falling. He was held by something greater in all his actions, both good and bad. Sin becomes irrelevant in relation to this new divine. A new morality compels one to integrate as much of the unconscious or the opposites that are God as one is able. This includes evil.

Jung remained concerned because of what he recognized as the limited consciousness-forming ability of humans, and therefore believed the actual transformation of evil takes place in the unconscious, through the changing symbols in relation to the God-image and the Self.

Their difference in thinking may be influenced by the fact that Jung was Christian while Neumann was Jewish. Neumann felt evil was capable of being recognized and possibly transformed, while Jung believed it was recognizably present yet largely not transformable, or left up to the Self in the unconscious. Neumann studied Jewish Mysticism and Kabbalistic teachings, that discuss how the most holy sparks are often to be found in the lowest, most impure thoughts and acts. Consciousness and one's ability to choose not to act in evil ways releases these sparks hidden in matter back to God. Goodness is released when one recognizes one's own evil residing in shadow, and God benefits or one could say the collective unconscious expands. There is no such belief in Christianity where evil and good are opposites split from one another and remain so according to the "old ethic." One's behavior is determined by a code of right and wrong rather than personal responsibility and choice.

What is Consciousness?

This idea led to an important shift in their discussion about whether God is unconscious or conscious. Jung seemed to suggest God is unconscious and needs humans in order for consciousness to be revealed. Neumann mused, "If we were the unconscious complexes of God that are endowed with consciousness and the possibility of consciousness, our task of consciousness and integration would also be sacred" (Jung & Neumann, 2015, p. 344, letter 118N). Neumann went further in wondering if humans' relationship to God is similar to all the cells and organisms that make up the human body. If so, he pondered, do the infinite small experiences of humans add up to absolute knowledge? What about the act of revelation, which Neumann wrote about from an historical Jewish perspective in the 1940s. It seems here that revelation reverses course, and humans, in contrast to common notions, enlighten God. With this possibility, both Jung and Neumann have arrived at similar conclusions.

Just a year and a half before his death, Neumann clarified his thinking in this discussion on the consciousness of God after reading Jung's chapter in *Memories, Dreams, Reflections* on "Life after Death and Late Thoughts" (Jung, 1989). If God incarnates in humans through likeness as an ego-Self, what is significant is that becoming conscious leads to the birth of the new divine. The creator and the Self create new experiences that did not exist beforehand. It is the ego-Self that carries the possibility for consciousness, for incarnation, and for change as it becomes conscious. Neumann referred to this as "the 'actualization of messianism' in individuation" (Jung & Neumann, 2015, p. 345, letter 118N). What is most relevant is the development of the individual, the conception of the archetype, and absolute knowledge as a counterpoint to Darwinist notions of haphazard transformations. The way to meaning and consciousness has not been found by accident but through the individual as the 'unit of salvation'" (2015, p. 346).

Returning to the problem of evil, Neumann proposed that: "The light wishes to illuminate, it creates dark bodies with the possibility that they will radiate light" (Jung & Neumann, 2015 p. 346, letter 118N). In other words, consciousness can emerge from either light or dark, good or evil. Our life experiences that generate consciousness come from both what we would consider creative as well as destructive. This may explain in part why, during the war, Neumann outrageously stated that the sacrifice of millions of Jews could result in a positive outcome for Jewish cultural development.

Two statements he made in the correspondence suggest he may have done something contrary to the prevailing morality, and in so doing felt he sinned for a greater good, namely his conscious development.[7] This goes back to the idea that each unique life lived contributes to God's consciousness. The ideas of evil and consciousness keep interweaving in their conversation, pointing to how closely connected they are.

We know that Jung lived according to the deep interior morality of the Self as opposed to the collective moral/ethical code of behavior. Jung, in response to Neumann, reminded him that the idea of the existence of a conscious God is not easily debated, pointing out that creation itself was a random, chaotic act of formless gas organizing itself into a circular order. He includes the creation of archetypes in this process. He explained that order is distinct from meaning and without humans there is no ability to detect meaning. Through creation the psychic (inner) and the physical (outer) are both present in the *psychoid*. Jung said, "It is through the archetype that we come closest to this early, irrepresentable, psychoid stage of conscious development; indeed, the archetype itself gives us direct intimations of it" (Jung & Neumann, 2015, p. 349-350, letter 119J). The psychoid is not psyche or matter alone but the neutral state of both together. Since we cannot conclude that the psyche, which is a higher synthesis, can emerge by chance alone, we need a hypothesis of latent meaning to explain it. Conversely, Jung said, "We do need the synchronistic experiences to be able to justify the hypothesis of a latent meaning that is independent of consciousness" (2015, p. 350). Synchronicity consists of acausal phenomena that can be seen as mere chance until meaning is attributed to them. The individual's own lived experience and awareness of something other is the point of conjunction between meaning and synchronicity.

Finally, Jung moved on to discuss two possibilities for the genesis of consciousness. One is that humans are attributed with a latent ability for reflective consciousness that gives humans a reason for being. The second is that latent meaning is attributed to the creator through a conscious plan of creation. If this last one is true, Jung wondered why the creator would bother creating such a plan when it already knows the outcome? Why should it create a second inferior consciousness alongside its omniscience? He puts it quite bluntly when he imagines, "billions of dull little mirrors of which he knows in advance what the picture will be like that they will reflect back" (Jung & Neumann, 2015, p. 350, letter 119J). Jung's conclusion from this exercise in logic and from the myth of the *incarnatio* was that God is similar to or the same as humans, in other words, as unconscious. For that reason, God felt compelled to become human and offer himself up for sacrifice to humans as a way to become conscious.

Conclusion

This was the end of the substance of Jung and Neumann's conversations. Neumann mentioned becoming ill in his last letter, September 1959 to Jung, and a year later he died, closely followed by Jung's death. They were both pondering the meaning of life and consciousness at the end of their lives, one coming from a Christian starting point and the other Jewish, which seemed to influence their perceptions. At this point in their lives, Jung was a tired old man, while in reading Neumann, the reader feels his pressure to make sense of life as death approached prematurely. I hope these two good friends were able to continue this discussion beyond the veil, wherever they are, perhaps with the advantage of the greater consciousness of God at their disposal. I certainly cannot include the increasing consciousness of humans, since life as it is playing out seems to dispute this possibility.

ENDNOTES

[1] Pardes means paradise, orchid, or garden. In the Talmud it refers to the dangers four sages have in entering the garden. One dies, another one loses his mind, the third one becomes a heretic, and the fourth one—Rabbi Akiva—enters and leaves the garden peacefully. Pardes serves as an acronym for the four levels of interpreting the Torah, from the concrete to the symbolic. The danger pertains to coming too close to God.

[2] Loewe, 2015, her paper in Turbulent Times, p. 396.

[3] Letter from Neumann to Jung, 66N, July 12, 1948, Analytical Psychology in Exile, p. 226.

[4] Her picture archive later became ARAS, Archive for Research in Archetypal symbolism. It is located at the C. G. Jung Institute of New York and is now online at www.aras.org,

[5] Jerome Bernstein, personal communication, 2011.

[6] In CW 10, par. 825-857.

[7] Neumann's first statement is: "To speak for myself, if I now fully or approximately understand the breaking in of the anima experience into my life (and my marriage)…" (Jung & Neumann, 2015, p. 92, letter 14N). The second statement is: "I have subsequently had to do "evil," for these images are to be fulfilled personally, but I did not experience it as a sin but as a necessary action. That has changed nothing in the suffering I have caused and into which I have fallen, but my feeling experience was different" (p. 332, letter 113N).

CHAPTER III

Analysis of *The Roots of Jewish Consciousness, Volume One: Revelation and Apocalypse*

Introduction

This two-volume work was not published in Neumann's lifetime, and he had no intention of publishing it, instead using it as resource material for his other books as well as his lectures. While this was his only full-length work on Jewish history and religious/spiritual development, it was here that he conceived some of the central concepts he later expanded on, such as the *ego-Self axis*, the archetype of the Great Mother, and *recollectivization*. Neumann's other work on a Jewish subject is *Jacob and Esau*.

He began work on *The Roots of Jewish Consciousness* after he fled Berlin in 1933 and Zurich in 1934, finishing Volume One in 1940 and Volume Two in early 1945. His focus at the time was on finding his own roots in his new land, reclaiming himself as a Jew and establishing himself as a Jungian analyst—exploring the world through these two lenses. His interest was on humanity's relation to God, revelation, consciousness, and good and evil. The anticipated volume three, which was to deal with the psychological understanding of this material, was never completed. Glimpses of the material that would have gone into that part are seen in the articles in the Appendices of Volumes One and Two and his other writings.

After the reality of the horrors that had transpired in Germany emerged at the end of the war, Neumann would no longer continue with this subject. It is also known that he told his good friend, Gustav Dreifuss, a Jungian analyst in Israel, that his background as a secular Jew who grew up in Germany was not sufficient to publish this material. He had relied on the work of Martin Buber for much of his source material, not on Gershom Scholem's work, even though he also lived in Israel. All three of these men were raised in Germany but Buber and Neumann continued to write in German, using source material written in German. Scholem, on the other hand, read and wrote in Hebrew and therefore had access to original Jewish source material.

At 28, a new immigrant in Palestine, amidst increasing horror and evil in the world, Neumann had descended into an introversion, writing in his new land to anchor himself and find his roots, and to understand the changing nature of life that includes good and evil. In a December 5, 1938 letter to Jung, Neumann described his project underway, also discussed in his work with Jung in 1933-1934:

> In the first part, I want to present how in Jewish antiquity the principle of direct revelation was valued, and how it stood in productive dialogue with the strong dependence of the people on earth and reality. The law as a secularization of the traumatic experience of exile, whereby, in the seeming acceptance of theocratic prophetism, the earth-principle asserted itself to the exclusion of direct revelation. Apocalypse, eschatological messianism (primitive Christianity). Gnosticism, as the emergence of the direct inner revelation that had been suppressed into a sideline. This is as far as I have gotten in the first draft.

He then described the second part:

> After a short chapter on the repression of direct revelation in the Talmud and the counter-movement in Kabbalah, there follows, as a comprehensive chapter, Hasidism. Religious renaissance of Judaism with the individual as a central phenomenon, but in collective constraint, through the enduring acceptance of the Law as a confining cage for direct revelation. (A course on this is already prepared in note form.) Assimilation and emancipation

> as a necessary de-collectivization of Jewish consciousness. Uprooting and the loss of memory.

Finally, he described his plan for the third part that he never completed, which is unfortunate because it sounds so interesting and pertinent:

> On the problem of the modern Jew. Using dream and fantasy material to illustrate the historic-collective connections. Reemergence of direct revelation, but now in the individual, in direct connection first with individuation and second with the collective problem of revelation in Judaism. Emergence of the earthly dimension as the location of revelation today—the converse of where the problem was located in Jewish antiquity—in a tension of opposites with the "spirit" principle that seems to hinder revelation. That is, while the revelation-principle used to stand opposed to the pagan earth-principle, now it arises positively paired with a strong Near Eastern Gnostic and pagan symbolism, in a strong tension of opposites with the Law. (Jung, Neumann, 2015, pp. 141; alt. trans from Briefe J-N, pp 189f)

We will discuss the first two parts. The third part is found as a profound influence in his later writings as he connected these understandings with the Jungian psychological process of individuation. As his grasp of Jewish history developed, his focus moved to the individual grounded on the earth with direct access to the divine and revelation emerging upward from the unconscious, as opposed to coming from the spirit down, as in earlier times. Neumann demonstrated his preference for prophesy over the priesthood as he moved into his second Volume on *Hasidism*.

One of his most poignant concepts has to do with good and evil, about which he wrote in his book, *Depth Psychology and the New Ethic,* and which emerges in many of his other writings. As Ann Lammers points out in Volume One of *The Roots of Jewish Consciousness*, "The unity of god and evil in God is a recurring theme in Hebrew scripture and Jewish tradition...as quoted in Isaiah 45:7, "I form the light, and create darkness; I make peace, and create evil; I am the LORD, that does these things" (Neumann, 2019a, p. xxxii). Jung has also quoted this passage from the Bible. While both men struggle with the reality of evil, each sees it somewhat differently as discussed in their correspondence. Neumann believed the ego had a greater share of moral responsibility for the transformation of evil, to redeem evil, while Jung felt evil was unconscious and ever-present. Yet in alchemy, the shadow must be made conscious and transformed. The ego becomes important for its stability in light of the choices it must make, leading Neumann to his concept of the ego-Self axis. In this book, he used this concept in relation to the YHWH-earth tension, the infinite versus the finite. He went on to give greater definition to this concept: the Self may displace the ego-complex but at the same time remain connected to it, creating the *I-Thou* relationship—that Martin Buber is so famous for—the ego and Self, I and God.

Neumann's Introduction to Roots

Tracing the mythical and historical world across cultures and religions, we can follow the development of the diversity of ideas leading to the evolution of human consciousness over time. As a means of understanding the commonalities and differences, Neumann drew from Jung and the concept of archetypal symbolism common to all humanity, though appearing in different ways. These unconscious images exert a formative influence on the conscious attitudes of individuals. Nevertheless, there is great variation in the way this universal human heritage is expressed. Neumann turns his focus specifically to the Jewish culture, which goes far back in history and was surrounded by a multiplicity of conflicting ideas and alternative religions as it developed. When he wrote this book during WWII, the Jewish situation had become catastrophic. The Jews had been assimilated into the Western world, even as it maintained a strong bias against the Old Testament and, consequently, anti-Semitic aggression against the Jews. At this time Christianity was meeting its pre-Christian, pagan roots through Gnosticism, Zoroastrianism, Near-Eastern religions and those that preceded the rise of consciousness and rationality. This movement clashed with the rootless and homeless Jew.

A review of history allows one to review the problem of the ancient Jew and what persists in the modern Jew from this past "The set of problems, as far as it is rooted in the Jewish collective unconscious, requires an in-depth study of the basic problems and contents affecting Jewish existence and its history" (Neumann, 2019a, p. 7). This problem is seen in the relationship between the unconscious and consciousness and how revelation developed from early Jewish culture up to today. Neumann leads us through the two great historical epochs giving us the background leading to the modern Jew. The first epoch in Jewish history represented the opposition between YHWH and the powers of nature, the YHWH-earth tension. This period included the apocalyptic writers and the psychic transformation that resulted from the destruction of the second temple. Christianity emerged later in this period as did Gnosticism. The second epoch Neumann writes about includes Hasidism, which was established in the late eighteenth-century and was a new approach to Judaism. Neumann's proposed third section would have focused on the existential problem of the modern Jew. Neumann pointed out that while Jewish character differs from those in ancient times, Judaism remained almost unchanged. This created a conflict and inner catastrophe for Neumann: "The plight of modern Jews— who like all modern humans lack direction, yet find themselves caught up in an age shaken to its foundations by catastrophes, lacking historical continuity, and plunged into a bottomless sociological pit—compels us to try to reconnect with the past in our own way" (2019a, p. 9). Neumann does this by reading a wide-ranging collection of Jewish texts with different interpretations. He studied diverse conceptions of history as well as observing the stories of the individual. His extensive lists of texts are listed in his bibliographies. Through his study, he attempts to reveal psychological attitudes, forms of psychic behaviors, and views of life related to the unconscious problem of modern Jews in his time. Neumann's hope was to find a way forward, shedding light on this dark path.

On The YHWH-Earth Relation and Prophecy

Moses and the revelation on Sinai is where Neumann begins his discussion of the early Jewish people. He sees the problem as their continuing possession by the earth and its fertility as opposed to spirit, represented by YHWH. This has remained a tension of opposites throughout history. Surrounding this early culture were the cults of the female deities, the Canaanites, those in Syria and Asia Minor. This represents nature's power over humans and the Great Mother's dominance over the patriarchy. The efforts of the Jews to overcome the dominance of the unconscious resulted in establishing an ego strong enough to withstand the regressive seductions of the Great Mother. This was not easily accomplished. To follow the biddings of the Father was dangerous, as the fire of light that reveals itself in revelation has the capacity to burn one up, "with his psychically invasive character, his catastrophically moving presence" (Neumann, 2019a, p. 22). The people instead preferred that Moses represent them and be the receiver and messenger of the revelations from YHWH in his fiery descent to the mountain. Moses, capable of withstanding the YHWH-earth tension, received the Tablets of the Law, the prophetic law and unifying symbol uniting himself and his people, spirit and matter. Unfortunately, the people were not capable of maintaining the tension between the earth and spirit and regressed to the Semitic orgiastic, fertility celebration of the Golden Calf. This was the counter-principle to YHWH as spirit, represented by the Tablets of the Law as prophetic law. Moses' intervention on behalf of his people prevented a catastrophe resulting from YHWH's rage and wrath against the violation of a taboo and the breaking of a covenant that could have resulted in a total annihilation of the people. There were three stages of action taken after this violation representing levels of consciousness. The first stage was the plague which represented the direct reaction of the collective unconscious from a biological level. The second was the ordeal where Moses' intervenes to support YHWH as the god who acts and judges. To support this stage of consciousness, an institutional figure representing the divinity was appointed, such as a priest or medicine man. This ordeal was not active on the biological level but instead was an intervention that has a judicial and ethical character. The final level was the trial that determined who stood with YHWH. Those who gathered around Moses dissolved the bond with the earth, severing natural ties, and strengthened their obedience to the inner voice representing the domain of YHWH. This resulted in the killing carried out by the Levites of three thousand people who did not stand with Moses. This third stage replaced the unconscious behavior of those killed in favor of conscious, ethical responsibility towards YHWH.

The weakness here among the Hebrews was fear and psychic inadequacy. Through this difficult process that began with failure and punishment, Moses was able to increase consciousness and obedience and dissolve the connection to the earth. In this Sinai experience he managed to turn his people into "a people." For his steadfast and dangerous work, Moses became the "Father of the Law" and a prophet—the true mana personality.

"The role of prophecy is the key to understanding the people's suspension between YHWH, on the one hand, and its natural involvement with the earth, on the other" (Neumann, 2019a, p. 36). With the emphasis now on spirit, the absence of the feminine fell back into the unconscious, into the earth as the Holy Land, *Eretz Israel*, and the Jewish soul (2019a, p. 41). This continuing involvement with the earth principle carries with it an undistorted view of good and evil. The spirit of god, the *Ruach breath,* is burning, restless energy, the light of illumination that can turn into militant affectivity or a destructively strong wind. It is, however, lasting, while the body-flesh/earth is transitory. YWHW is the god of the distance and also the god of fertility, but not of the earth. Yet, it is a god that takes blood in sacrifice from the body that belongs to the earth.

Neumann proceeded to discuss the nature of prophecy as it relates to mysticism and divination for the individual. The experience can be self-reflecting or ego-dissolving. The greater the difference between conscious awareness and the content being revealed, the greater the danger. Revelations that occur in dreams and visions emerge in limited states of consciousness and are considered of lesser value than the true revelation that bears no connection to the ego-complex. The closer to the ego the content is, the more connection it has to the subjective personality, while further away, the more objective it is. "A true prophet is only someone to whom are whispered the contents of the collective unconscious, the inherent activity of which determines the historical process. This is the deepest foundation for the idea of YHWH as the God who determines history" (Neumann, 2019a, p. 48).

What is required of the prophet is ego-stability, which means not surrendering to the contents of the unconscious but resisting them, to see clearly and maintain stability of consciousness in the face of unconscious contents that threaten to dissolve the ego. Maintaining a moral stance requires the same ego-stability. A tension is constituted between the ego consciousness and the unconscious, while the revelation is held in between the two as the transcendent function. Here it corresponds to YHWH's specific nature of a moral, law giving God, which when revealed strengthens consciousness. Moses' capacity to hold the tension between YHWH and the people demonstrates his ego-stability to stand at the midpoint between the two and act as the mediator. At times in history, prophets had to intervene for the benefit of the people, to present their case, such as Abraham bargaining with YHWH to save Sodom and Gomorrah. Yet these prophets fundamentally remain YHWH's instruments to correct the people. "The issue here is not individual salvation, but the collective salvation of the *Bnei* Israel summoned by YHWH" (Neumann, 2019a, p. 56).

What subsequently developed was a priesthood that created laws that no longer needed further revelations. Until the destruction of the second temple, the tension between the prophetic and priests remained. Much of this was driven by the need for secularized laws to establish a secure social and national culture. And yet the covenant partnership between YHWH and Israel remained ever-present, demonstrated in the ritual of circumcision and Passover:

> YHWH's irruptive revelation, remains always and unconditionally dominant over the system of consciousness and ego. Ego and YHWH are partners. This configuration, however, includes in itself the living polarity of the relationship between YHWH and earth,

> and the polarity of consciousness and the unconscious. This is both the assertion and the attitude of revelation. (Neumann, 2019a, p. 61)

Part of this partnership is seen in YHWH changing directions when his people do, maintaining a dynamic view of the reciprocity that existed between them. "No situation is so forlorn that YHWH, given this incalculable domain, could not intervene and change it because he is the Lord. But likewise, no situation is so secure that it could not be fundamentally overturned in an instant by his catastrophic irruption" (2019a, p. 62).

Neumann pointed out that the Hebrews were the only Semites to not have a female deity. Her energy, capable of influencing fertility, life and fate, remained in the background poised to flood consciousness, which it did on many occasions.

On The Apocalypse: Heightening the YHWH-Earth Tension

As Israel became embedded as a historical people with the political and economic realities of life in the Middle East, it became more secularized as the Jews tried to fit in. In doing so, the people moved further away from the early Jewish principles and the rule of YHWH. With this shift, the YHWH-earth tension grew. After the destruction of the First Temple and the Babylonian exile, the peoples' communal covenant with YHWH, regarding the power of prophesy and YHWH's ascendency over existence, was lost (Neumann, 2019a, p. 76). Previously, the individual was part of a communal whole, a tribal confederacy with a shared fate. Now the individual was separated and released into his own destiny. This followed the example of Ezekiel 18:20:

> The soul that sins shall die. The son shall not suffer for the iniquity of the father, nor the father suffer for the iniquity of the son; the righteousness of the righteous shall be upon himself, and the wickedness of the wicked shall be upon himself. (Alter, 2018, p. 1101)

Nevertheless, Neumann pointed out that later cultural events, specifically WWII, once again threw the individual back into the collective. Understanding this in psychological terms, Neumann discussed the back and forth movement between the two opposing developments—the collective group versus the individual. This can be observed throughout history and especially after a catastrophe. The highly differentiated individual finds his way back to the collective, while the less conscious and less differentiated, experiencing suffering, begin to feel and think for the first time, leading to greater differentiation.

With the establishment of the Second Temple and the legal-priestly tradition emphasizing cultural form through the law, the theocratic principle fell to the individual. As the earth became more remote and dangerous, divinity was perceived as retreating and prophecy officially ended. To compensate, prophecy was projected to the end of days and apocalyptic perspectives—the vision of what is at work behind the visible world—became more prevalent:

> Ordinary religious life was increasingly forced away from the official line of priestly theocracy and toward the individual. But, in addition, these small groups, as we know, were the seedbed of the new religious movements that found their visible expressions in apocalypticism and early Christianity. (Neumann, 2019a, p. 78)

The apocalyptic viewpoint asserts "a process of historical decadence, progressively declining under the rule of evil" (Neumann, 2019a, p. 79). The individual was responsible for maintaining a strong sense of ethics and consciousness, carrying righteousness and unrighteousness alone. This led to guilt and repression, resulting in an activation of the unconscious. The present being so oppressive and dark, to avoid suffering the guilt, salvation was projected toward the prophetic apocalypse at the end of time. This shift toward the Last Judgment reflects the belief that the YHWH-earth tension cannot be resolved. Instead, salvation is pushed forward into future history, as the fulfillment of a plan. The world can fill with evil but the plan will take place at its right time. This allowed a sense of hope and redemption in the belief that YHWH will intervene to save his people and the world. This event is not an intrapsychic event but is a projection out into world of YHWH's killing word, his deadly storm or consuming fire (Neumann, 2019a, p. 87):

> YHWH's paradoxical nature here becomes the knowledge of a law by which this paradox is overcome, a law by which the possibility of miracle and liberation is always greatest just at the moment when all rational orientation fails, and consciousness no longer sees any escape but doom. (Neumann, 2019a, p. 84)

Neumann discussed how the birth of Christ was a turning point in world history, closely related to the apocalyptic movement in Judaism. The Last Judgment was reconceived as the necessity of death for all rebirth. This new Eon refers to the rebirth and renewal of the world and all its inhabitants through divine revelation. The effect was that YWHW moved far up and away while humanity moved down, creating a larger split between the two that only a complete transformation will resolve. As the Satanic dark element was more visible, the messiah had to be of equal power:

> YHWH, himself, the creator of heaven and earth before time began, the creator of the very principle of opposites, guarantees the synthesis and keeps it safe "with him." YHWH, as the earth's opposite polarity, enables to some extent the historical process that is energized by the principle of opposites. He does so by occupying one of the poles, but not by becoming dualistically identical with it, or by being dissolved into the pair of opposites. (Neumann, 2019a, p. 90)

The idea of the messiah emerged as the son of God, the Chosen One, and the son of man as a unifying symbol and also the transcendent function reconciling the heaven-earth opposition while the perfection of the first creation is restored. The Hidden Light of the first day of creation represents the original knowledge or "the primordial wisdom of the collective unconscious" (Neumann, 2019a, p. 93). Neumann gave a clear interpretation of the psychological eschatology behind this significant compensatory shift. He also compared apocalypse to alchemy—the difference is between a collective transformation as opposed to individual development in alchemy. As Lord of history, YHWH controls time, both present time and future time. Rebirth comes at the end of time when the earth-heaven opposition returns to balance and creation is restored. "The time component [is seen in the] unconscious background factors, which move toward actualization over the course of time, revealing themselves as determiners of reality" (Neumann, 2019a, p. 99). Neumann hinted at his thoughts for part three of this work by comparing the prophetic experience of YHWH with the psychology of the introverted intuitive type with undeveloped sensation, which can lead to a difficulty for that individual to remain grounded in reality. Similarly, this theology effectively presents catastrophes as temporary obstacles on the path to eventual bliss, which effectively hollows out existence where reality becomes a permanently provisional attitude.

On The Dangerous Ending of the YHWH-Earth Tension

The YHWH-earth tension in early Judaism is compared to Gnosticism—which believes that the vessel of God shattered with the creation of the world and the shards of consciousness or knowledge fell into the world and the unconscious. The Gnostic task is to gather all the shards and return them to the vessel "to achieve as a reality the human being's original state of belonging to the world of higher consciousness, the realm of light" (Neumann, 2019a, p.116). When the gathering of light comes from above, it is an act of redemption that goes into the unconscious. Gnosticism lays out the danger to ego consciousness from this type of redemption. The light can easily be overwhelmed by the unconscious, resulting in the regression of the individual personality. It is not about universal redemption but about what the individual can remember and make conscious of those contents that were once conscious in the original world of light. These are the latent conscious qualities that exist to some extent in the unconscious (2019a, p.116). The shards of light once rescued, return to where light originated, with the deity. Neumann points out that this is similar to all mystery religions where there is redemption of the ego through the Self. In Gnosticism as in Manichaeism, ego consciousness is transformed, not the psyche as a whole. The dark, evil parts are not transformed. They are merely isolated, and therefore, the problem of the inferior side and the opposites is not resolved.

The goal in Gnosticism is to dissolve the ego into the Self, moving from below to above, which abandons the world. This is unacceptable to Judaism, which is interested in redemption *in* the world not out of it. Judaism attributes the world to be a divine creation, with a purity of nature. What is negative in the divine creation is inherent in human beings. Therefore, the Jew takes on the responsibility for evil, holding the tension between good and evil. In Gnosticism and Christianity evil is seen in the flesh, in the feminine, and in nature where the devil is lord, but this is not the case in Judaism. The power of evil as understood in Judaism is an instrument in the hand of YHWH, the lord of the whole world with his two-sidedness. Original sin does not exist and freedom of choice remains possible for the individual. Corruption and sinfulness arise from the body's instinctiveness, from the dark, chaotic waters of the unconscious. "Unlike Gnosticism, it does not make an extra-human intervention for the sake of humanity the indispensable prerequisite of redemption" (Neumann, 2019a, p. 120). Judaism does not resolve the YHWH-earth tension but rather maintains a structure that includes both, a world with both light and darkness.

Now that revelation had abated, the original covenant between YHWH and the people was converted into the development of the *Halakha* and Talmud, the laws and regulations of conduct and rational intellect. This fulfilled the need to focus on survival during the continuing exiles and continued to hold the group together. "Only the old revelation was valid....But the destruction of the collective foundation now led to a violent recollectivizing, for this alone made it possible for the people to go on existing" (Neumann, 2019a, p.128). In this masculinization, consciousness and unconsciousness moved further apart in the *Galut* Jew, while the shadow of the repressed mother-archetype in the form of *Lilith* the demonic seducer, seeped through to prevent the development of consciousness. Yet, the mother archetype retained its vitality in relation to the earth or Israel, and provided a counterweight to "YWHW's fatherly claim, as a complementary pair of forces" (Neumann, 2015a, p, 131). Although as Neumann pointed out, she "crept secretly, thus doubly dangerously, into the purely masculine world of Judaism" (2019a, p. 131). The rule of the mother archetype began with her infantilizing, nurturing, intoxicating, castrating, concretizing tendencies, preventing the expansion of consciousness:

> This separation, corresponding psychologically to the dissociation of consciousness from the primal creative powers of the collective unconscious, was expressed symptomatically within Judaism by the exclusion of direct religious expression and also by the provisional paralysis of adherence to the law. (Neumann, 2019a, p. 133)

Now with the introduction of Hasidism, which was an anti-Gnostic movement, the feminine as the *Shekhinah*, the bride of God, the indwelling presence of God in Israel and the earth-archetype, returned to consciousness.

On The Author's Appendices

1. On *Methodology*

This first paper describes the biblical texts as being psychologically real experiences that have been worked on and worked through, while at the same time they contain genuine psychic phenomena that is of interest. The symbolic elements give information about the lived events. Neumann favored "a structural interpretation that analyzes events and the attitudes evident in them. For this psychological interpretation, cultural-historical and historical aspects are primary, but in addition, the relationship between conscious and unconscious is also central" (Neumann, 2019a, p. 138).

2. On *The Foundation Stone and the Waters of the Deep*

Neumann explored in this paper Midrashic texts about the foundation stone and the waters of the deep in relation to the struggle establishing consciousness through the law, as the stone that binds the chaotic waters of the dangerous unconscious. The stone, which is the seal of YHWH, "has two functions: it locks the mouth of the abyss preventing the waters of the deep from gushing up and creating chaos; and it forms the navel of the world, upon which stand the Ark of the Covenant in the Holy of Holies...or lie as subterranean seals in the foundation of the Temple" (Neumann, 2019a, p. 141).

This conflict of opposites—the duality of the world, good and evil, above and below, right and left, consciousness and the unconscious—is secured by the cap stone to keep the two poles separate to prevent the flooding of the world. This reflects the psychological understanding of the fundamental relationship between consciousness and the unconscious. One needs a strong enough ego or collective laws to prevent flooding, which would result in regression or the "sacred death" of being carried off by the divine rather than transforming (Neumann, 2019a, p. 143).

One final interesting point that Neumann made has to do with God's grace in the Old Testament, which he said is misunderstood in Christianity (2019a, p. 144). It has to do with "Moses preventing YHWH's wrath from destroying the whole people, and the subsequent theophany of God's grace" (Neumann, 2019a, p. 144). This points to the significant reciprocal relationship that exists between humans and YHWH. Humans, that is, Moses and Abraham, caused God to behave in a different way by containing his wrath. It also speaks to how humans play a role in helping God become more conscious. This dynamic is also seen in *Answer to Job*.

3. On *The Composition of the Pentateuch*

There was a competition between two early groups of followers of Moses both positioning themselves to be historically relevant. "But, as the early prophetic structure of the texts has remained unrecognized until now, the only textual revision emphasized was the one that introduced the priestly Zadokite element into the text, in order to subordinate the Levitical element (Neumann, 2919a, p. 144). Neumann traced historical revisions primarily by early reviser/redactor Abiathar, regarding conflicts and differences between prophecy versus codified ritual, reflecting the differences and similarities between the Levite and Aronite-Zadokite priests. "The battle [was] between the Levites and the Aronite-Zadokite priests, who both oppose the prophetic conception of YHWH's direct charismatic choice" (Neumann, 2019a, p. 144, n.27). This struggle between prophetic tendencies and counter-tendencies reflects the original struggle between Moses and the people.

4. On The *Earth and the Symbols of the Elements*

This appendix explores five archetypal themes related to the YHWH-earth conflict: Wind, Body-soul and Blood, Earth and Bull, Circumcision and Passover, and Lilith. The material from the midrashic texts comes from different periods, historical contexts and foreign influence, but what is important here for Neumann is the pervasiveness of the symbolism and its historical impact (Neumann, 2019a, p. 150).

On *Wind Symbolism*

"Everything comes into being only through unification and opposition" (Neumann, 2019a, p. 148). This is true for the elements of wind-fire which oppose earth-water. Wind and water were present before creation as the wind of the Lord of creation hovered above the water. Wind implies wisdom, which is symbolically connected to *Sophia*, the daughter of wind, the Holy Spirit with whom she is identified. Wind-breath-soul-*ruach* connects the basic opposites of consciousness and the unconscious and gives meaning to them. "The position of wind between heaven and earth corresponds at every point to the position of the *Shekhinah* between YHWH and the world...and that of Israel between YHWH and the peoples (2019a, p. 150).

On *The Body-Soul and Blood*

Nefesh is the flesh and blood soul, where the blood belongs to the earth and is given as sacrifice in circumcision, or in animal sacrifice, for example.

There is a cooperation between YHWH and the earth as it reacts to YHWH's law. The earth can turn against sinners who go against the earthly justice of YHWH's laws.

Neumann explained the difference between the five parts of soul elaborated upon in the Kabbalah which were already written about in the midrash. "*Nefesh* as the principle of blood and life, vitality, earth, located in the liver; *ruach* as the ascending and descending principle of wind and spirit, and *neshama* as the rational soul, both represent rationality located in the heart; *yehida* as the unitary soul in contrast to the polarity of the body; and *haya* as the soul of life, which ascending in sleep, draws life from above" (Neumann, 2019a, p. 152). The opposition between *ruach* and *nefesh* mirrors the opposition between YHWH and earth. While body, earth and nature were subordinated to YHWH throughout Jewish history, in Genesis, *ruach*, the breath of life, was prominent.

On *The Earth and Bull*

Adam in Genesis ruled over the earth or soil named *adama*. The curse that struck him also struck the earth, which remained a threat. In the midrash, the earth was second to YHWH and in cooperation with it. Earth ruled the outer world of day and sunlight, while YHWH ruled the inner world of night and sleep, revelation and the soul. The people were held in the middle of the polarity until they moved towards earth and, for example, the Golden Calf. Polarity was lost in the *participation mystique* with the earth, where the calf and/or bull are prominent archetypal symbols of earth's fertility. These animals emerge in numerous mystery religions, including Mithraic, Dionysian, Shiva's bull, and those of the early Great Mother, Cybele.

On *Circumcision and Passover*

Neumann attempted to make a connection between circumcision and Passover as YHWH uses blood to make a connection between the earth-body aspect and spirit. Blood is the mediator between the two, hence, becoming a substance of the body but also of spirit. "YHWH attacks Moses immediately after his return from Egypt, because the latter had neglected his son's circumcision" (Neumann, 2019a, p. 155). During this procedure blood pays a vital role sealing the wedding rite to YHWH—YHWH's marriage with Israel. Moses' child was circumcised by his mother, Zipporah, and he became the "bridegroom of blood" (2019a, p. 176). The covenant is secured and Moses is protected against YHWH's negative forces. Circumcision protects the individual, especially from Lilith, just as the Passover ritual protects the people. This ritual was originally an adolescent initiation into the collective. Only those who are united in the circumcision covenant with YHWH are included in YHWH's collective union with the people.

On *Lilith*

Lilith is the negative feminine principle, the child eater and female demon. The circumcision rite as a puberty rite was a means of protecting young males from the evils and seductions of the Terrible Great Mother:

> Until puberty, the child, the male child as well, has lived largely within the motherly domain, and its very life is assigned to the sphere of women. One essential purpose of puberty rites is to dissolve the participation mystique between mother and son, and thus to make him inwardly capable of sexuality. In the process, his childhood can be ended, the feminine imago can be separated from the mother, and the liberated image of the feminine can now be projected onto a same-age female partner. (Neumann, 2019a, p. 157)

Lilith was Adam's first wife, the feminine aspect of the deity, yet the one who is the lowest and most impure, representing the waning moon, the queen of the demons, feminine aspect of Satan, the embodiment of sexual desire and fornication, profoundly hostile towards men and dangerous to children. She is connected with blood and menstruation. "Lilith is the blood from the cleansing [of the blood] of the Shekhinah" (2019a, p. 159). The Shekhinah is the full bright moon, the positive anima-aspect of the feminine, while Lilith is the dark moon, the negative anima. As Adam's first wife it was written:

> When the Holy One had created the first human being, he said: it is not good for man to be alone. And so he made him a wife from the earth (*adama*), like unto him, and called her Lilith. They immediately started quarrelling. She said: "I do not want to lie below." But he said: "I do not want to lie below, but on top, and it befits you to be below, and me on top." She said, "We are equal, because we both come from the earth," and neither wanted to obey the other. When Lilith realized this, she spoke the *Shem ha-Meforash*, God's unspeakable name and flew into the air of the world. (Neumann, 2019a, p. 162)

Lilith is an adversary of consciousness and a profound threat because of her sexual, magical practices that drag one into the perverse world of instincts, to the early pagan level, the negative domain of earth, and of the unconscious leading to a self-poisoning of the soul. This is in complete contrast to YHWH's laws of cleanliness, circumcision, and sexuality leading to procreation and to cooperation with the earth. Lilith's demand to be on top is completely rejected. She is "the real adversary of consciousness and its most profound threat" (Neumann, 2019a, p. 163).

CHAPTER IV

Analysis of *The Roots of Jewish Consciousness, Volume Two: Hasidism* and its Psychological Meaning for Judaism

Introduction to Volume Two

Erich Neumann wrote and finished the second volume, *The Roots of Jewish Consciousness: Hasidism* in 1945, as news of the horrors of Nazi death camps and Jewish liberation was being widely released. He put this work aside and did not continue with his formerly proposed part three that would have integrated this material with psychology. He did, though, write four papers, included in the appendix of this text, on the importance of consciousness in the experience of depth psychology, integrating his material with Jungian depth psychology. As seen in these books and papers, Neumann seeks to understand human development, the nature of good and evil, masculine and feminine, and the path towards spiritual and psychological wholeness. To this end, Neumann used as a primary resource Martin Buber's writings and understanding of Hasidism and Kabbalah, among others.

The chapter "Life in this World," describing the paradox of good and evil as both being contained in God—that good can be attributed to evil events— was removed from the text for unknown reasons. Perhaps it was too difficult to include in the wake of the Holocaust. The writing was not as refined as the other chapters. Perhaps while in process he sent it to others to read and comment on, and for unknown reasons did not include it in his fair copy. It is understandable that this material would become very difficult. Neumann did include many of the themes and insights, such as ego-Self axis and the paradoxical unity of good and evil, from *The Roots of Jewish Consciousness* into later books he completed and published after the war: *Depth Psychology and a New Ethic* and *Origins and History of Consciousness*. The aforementioned four papers included in the appendix, written between 1942-1943, also include many of Neumann's novel ideas. His concepts of primary and secondary personalization and further elaboration of his understanding of developmental psychology can be seen here. They are interesting papers.

On The Structure of the World as Inwardness

Neumann offers a depth-psychological interpretation of the historical development of the Jewish person's psychic structure, leading up to and seen in Hasidism. With the disintegration of the Jewish collective, the inward-focused/introverted/meditative attitude of the individual coalesced into the spiritual movement of Hasidism. Its focus was on the original Kabbalistic and Hasidic principle of creation, *tzimtzum* or God's self-contraction, and its continuing affirmation by humanity. Because of his love, God contracted himself so that his brilliance could be received by humans. Through this process, every individual is unique and strives to bring his character to perfection, influencing others and the collective to achieve the same ends. "Based on the tension produced by the ineradicable difference between God and humankind, these opposites begin to be synthesized, and thereby confer on humanity an ever-greater depth and an increasingly stronger capacity for illumination" (Neumann, 2019b, p. 6). Yet, while humans remain imperfect, the coming of the messiah is delayed.

The *tzaddikim* are the wise teachers, "the doctors of the soul" (Neumann, 2019b, p.8) who hold the individual's divine vessel that receives the revelation of the teachings, allowing the messianic development of the soul. Through this process, the hidden sparks of light found everywhere are redeemed by the souls to which they belong:

> His task *not* as being an advocate, but as awakening the central activity of the individual and leading him to that layer from which the individual's religious autonomy creatively breaks through. The *tzaddik* must help the individual to conduct his

> never-ending conversation with the divine in his own voice—not the borrowed voice of the tzaddik. (2019b, p. 10)

The human becomes the redemptive bridge between divinity and the world, through individuation and wholeness. Holding the opposites in consciousness, results in creative rebirth out of nothingness. No one is considered perfect or has achieved divine wholeness until he or she has resolved the opposites of masculine and feminine, heaven above and the earth below:

> Only if a single eye of humanity could be formed from the immense number of human individualities, in their endlessly varied capacity for experience, might that unified eye alone recognize the hidden light of the world diamond. Only such a unified humanity would be the partner for a self-revealing world. (Neumann, 2019b, p.16)

It is interesting that Neumann, in this quote, referred to the single eye of humanity, similar to the single eye of God that opened in his forehead in his vision of the ape-man. He is processing this material deeply. This description leads to the concept of the "actualizing of messianism" (Neumann, 2019b, p. 18) which refers to the turning away from the future to the present, from the outside to the inside where messianism is a stage in the individual's development—to realize one's Elijah soul. Everything relies on human choice. The key here is that everyone, collective humanity, must reach this stage, not just a few. Neumann discusses the concepts of the Kabbalah, the *Sefirot* of the tree of life, containing the Holy sparks, which influenced Hasidism, including the soul, the *sekel as* an organ of the transpersonal associated with *neshama,* reason and consciousness (Neumann, 2019b, p.26).

The problem of evil is prominent in the Kabbala. If there is no evil, there would be no good for they are opposite sides of each other. But what is evil?

> The problem of evil is many sided. Whether evil is seen as overflowing from the judging and punishing power, where it exists as a counter hierarchy of impurity, fed by human sin, whether it is said to be the vestige of primordial worlds that existed before our world, and thus represents the husks of the world tree, whether evil is seen as waste products of the world organism or as the distancing of the creature from the divine, each of these views can be understood by depth psychology, because within the psyche each of these aspects is experienced as evil, and as real. (Neumann, 2019b, p.30)

As evil confronts good, humans have the ability to reject evil and choose good instead, a victory for good. It is related to the problem of Lilith and the tension between YHWH and the earth. Yet, it is evil that creates the energetic tension between the opposites, creating motivation in the unconscious to develop a differentiating consciousness. Because the sparks exist in everything, God participates along with the individual in the transformation of evil: "The point is not simply that God *also* exists in uncleanness, but that he is *especially* there. For: The holiest sparks exist on the lowest levels" (Neumann, 2019b, p. 46-47).

On The Transformation of Souls

This chapter deals with the essential understanding of Hasidism and what it derived from Kabbalah, whose system of meaning is described in detail and compared to the symbolic level in depth psychology. The theory of redemption of humans and the world, through the reclamation of sparks of light in the human soul vessel, understands divinity as nothingness or Wisdom. The redemption is an inner revelation from the unconscious:

> Revelation is a kindling, inflammatory process, in which the human soul and the spark of that thing that is pregnant with revelation unite, collide, and procreate. The spark's will to be redeemed, and the soul's to redeem, are two matching and cross-fertilizing directions in the world's dynamic...nothing is

> perfect that is not simultaneously masculine and feminine. (Neumann, 2019b, p. 60)

The sparks transform themselves becoming more transparent, and in the process change the individual and the world.

The path of introversion/meditation progresses through the four stages of the world, i.e., mineral, vegetable, animal, and human, and through the ten *sefirot* of the Kabbalah. Each *sefirah* is an archetype with its own unique energy. The image of the human being is projected onto the sefirotic world in the form of the higher, primordial human, *Adam Kadmon,* who sits in *Tiferet,* the king or sun, at the center of the tree of life. It is here that all opposites are brought together, along with the three parts of the soul, *neshama, ruach* and *nefesh,* and where words and meaning find expression in divinity. *Adam Kadmon* unites with his opposite, the *Shekhinah,* the feminine aspect of God, and the union is represented psychologically as the Self. "The Self is a result of the connection of *ruach,* with *nefesh* and *neshama*. That is, it results from individuation within the human being, as a process leading to wholeness" (Neumann, 2019b, p. 83). This wholeness is manifested through the *tzaddik,* who supports the central task of "working on God's human form" (2019b, p. 85).

On Life in this World

Contrasts are made between Hasidism and Jewish intellectualism and the rabbinical ideal of knowledge. Hasidism is movement as seen in, "one who walks, opposed to the safe and rigid path of knowledge and its righteousness" (Neumann, 2019b, p. 90). It values a passion for life, change, and constant renewal. Quotes from Hasidic texts are used to express important understandings concerning unknowing and belief, joy and wholeness, love and fear, the feminine principle, the teaching of the soul, repentance, the introversion of sacrifice, evil as a level of good, the serpent of paradise, accepting the world, and the world as symbol.

Some concepts are as follows: the divine sparks are found at the lowest levels; joy shows a closeness to God and leads to goodness; there is holiness in the simplicity of belief. One of Neumann's ideas that stands out was his observation that polar opposition of masculine and feminine changed in Kabbalah and Hasidism, becoming strikingly similar to Jungian psychology's developments understanding masculine and feminine/ anima and animus duality. This is also seen, more broadly, in gender ideas today. "It is clear that the inwardness of the male is female, and the inwardness of the female is male" (Neumann, 2019b, p. 130):

> Previously, even in the Kabbalah, marriage was seen as the union of two sexual polarities to form a hermaphroditic, transindividual being, which still consist in two persons. In contrast, when the parts of the soul are united, this process is introjected within one individual. Here, based on the model of Adam Kadmon, male and female combine within one individual to form a whole. This means, however, that a new image of the human being begins to constellate itself, one no longer centered on polarized sexuality, but instead on Adam Kadmon's hermaphroditic character. (2019b, p. 97)

In Hasidism, humans, always moving and changing, can repent their wrong actions and thoughts and turn towards holiness. "Actualization places the individual at the center of destiny, for the world and for God" (Neumann, 2019b, p. 103). It is up to humans to choose the right path. The experience of evil is unavoidable, but through human choice, goodness may be revealed and one may becomes more conscious. As an integral part of this world, it is vitally important to accept it for what it is. "The whole world is pregnant with revelation, waiting to become visible and reveal its inner, hidden light." (2019b, p.112) The *tzaddik,* as the whole human being, is the template for what others aspire to become.

On The Human Being and the New Image of God

Aspects of the *tzaddik* are examined, from his hiddenness from the world and therefore closeness to God and nothingness, to later views of his becoming an inflated mana-personality. The *tzaddik* oversees the world and assists humans in recognizing and redeeming their inner soul sparks.

He has realized his universal human core, as the Self represented by *Adam Kadmon* as *Tiferet* in the world. He has traversed the three developmental stages of the world of ego, mother and father, and the three ages of youth, middle age and old age. Having done so, he reclaimed his own light, the soul, and the Self as wholeness. These ages correspond to the three souls, *nefesh, ruach*, and *neshama.*

In Hasidism as in individuation, through spiritual development, the focus shifts from the ego to the Self as unity and wholeness at the center of the personality. All opposites coalesce into the whole, including good and evil, as YHWH is both good and evil. Hasidism and Gnosticism are compared. While both advocate redeeming divine sparks, in Hasidism the task is up to humans to make the world holy by bringing the immanence and wisdom of God, the *Shekhinah,* into the world. The human being is where divine power unfolds, the bridge between the world and God, transforming all three and releasing God's grace into the world.

On Hasidism and the Birth of the Modern Jew

The prevailing mysteries of the Near East before and at the time of early Christianity concerned the dying and resurrecting son-deities and the incarnate god. Both these themes were united in the concept of Christ. Judaism expressed these mysteries as the introversion of the messiah, a unifying symbol of heaven and earth, which Christianity then concretized in the historical form of the figure of Jesus as the Christ, the center of the redemptive event. In response, Judaism recollectivized itself, returning to its belief in dogma and rabbinism. This path was reversed with the introduction of Kabbalah and Hasidism, which included belief in outer redemption through the *tzaddkim,* and in inner redemption and wholeness through the inner messiah figure of *Adam Kadmon.* The history of individual destiny replaced the collective history of the world.

The later decline of Hasidism resulted in a return to rabbinism. Loss of collective memory of Jewish psychic roots and assimilation into the Western world have influenced the psychology of modern Jews. This loss of connection to the deep collective layer created a blindness that also obscured the activation of a gruesome and primal fire of destruction. These losses have left the modern Jew in a state of neurosis.

In the symbol of Adam Kadmon, Neumann explored and solidified his thinking about ethics and morality as presented in his book, *Depth Psychology and the New Ethic:*

> Adam Kadmon's demand that every individual actualize his unrepeatable wholeness, with the result that tradition and the certainty of knowledge becomes relative. The relativizing of ethical values—pure and impure, good and evil, knowing and unknowing—is expressed in the principle of 'good uncertainty.' And the tradition of 'the merits of the fathers' is also abolished, for what is needed is one's own light and the new revelation. At the same time, the principle of reward and punishment, which supports morality, is also abolished because repentance, the transformation of human beings, which may and must occur at any time, creates an ever-new relationship between humanity and God, consciousness and unconscious." (2019b, p. 176)

The book ended with further discussion of the modern Jew of his time, and the decline of Hasidism with its memory loss and regression back to the rationalism of rabbinism. There were no restraints to the process of Jews assimilating into and secularizing in 19th century Europe:

> The grand delusion, which would lead Jews, especially in the twentieth century, to the brink of absolute despair, is also symptomatic of a loss of their own instinctive foundation.
>
> Only the passionate longing to have finally reached the shores of a peaceful and unbarbaric world explains the terrible blindness with which the Jews hurled themselves into the deadly light of deception by the west, a light that, in the annihilation of European Jewry, became a gruesome beacon for the victory of the primal fire, which nothing human has tamed. (Neumann, 2019b, p. 178)

Conclusion

As Neumann descended into his study of his roots in Judaism from the historical past to his present in his new land of Palestine, we see the development of his ideas on certain themes that repeat over his lifetime of work. In the four papers included in the appendix B of Volume Two of *The Roots of Jewish Consciousness*, he took up a comparison of Hasidism and Kabbalah with depth psychology. It is likely that these papers were part of the final volume of the book he originally intended to write. When he abandoned the book in 1945 at the end of the war, he moved away from religious study to focus on topics such as ethics, the nature of evil, consciousness, and the stages of life from a depth psychological perspective. Rather than summarize those four early papers (1942-1943), we find similar themes expressed with greater clarity and examination in his book, *The Origins of History and Consciousness*. The papers are nevertheless worth reading for reference:

Appendix B consists of these four papers dealing with the importance of consciousness in the experience of depth psychology:

1. Symbols and stages of conscious development
2. The development of consciousness and the stages of life
3. The path of depth psychology and consciousness
4. The religious meaning of the path of depth psychology

CHAPTER V

Analysis of *The Origins and History of Consciousness*, and Its Precursors

On Neumann's Introduction

Perhaps Erich Neumann's most recognizable book, *The Origins and History of Consciousness* has been in print since 1949. In this book he lays out the stages of individual development that parallel the emergence of collective human consciousness. Myths reflecting common archetypal themes and behaviors are the stories and images of the process that takes place in the human psyche. The psyche strives for consciousness out of the original unitary reality of chaos, establishing through *centroversion* the ego-Self axis, and unifying itself once again through the process of individuation. Thus are the conscious and unconscious realms brought back into a whole.

As mentioned earlier, Neumann spent his years before and during WWII on the material in this book, first laying out his thoughts in other manuscripts that have now been published, shedding light on his thinking process and the development of his ideas. Many of his interests and important contributions emerged in these early documents. Through them, we have the privilege of watching his mind/psyche/feeling experiences develop and clarify into what is a rare precious gift for us all. Neumann brilliantly laid out the psychological process of human development following the psyche's course through centroversion and individuation, and also when it remains unlived, neurotic or regressed. He is the rare Jungian who focuses his attention on the regressive theories of Freud and Alfred Adler, explaining clearly what in them is useful and where they are wrong. While Jung focused on the second half of life, Neumann started at the beginning. Neumann kept his eye on the healthy development of the personality, not ignoring any stage. He moved from the mystical in *Creative Man* (Neumann, 1979) back to *The Child* (Neumann, 1973), his last book, completed by his wife Julia after his death.

Neumann established a unifying overview of the psyche from infancy onward. Jung believed that Neumann "arrives at conclusions and insights, which are among the most important ever to be reached in this field," noting that "only in retrospect does the pioneer know what he needed to know before" (Jung, p. xiv in Neumann, 1949).[1] Neumann's theory rejects Freud's biologically based developmental theory, which does not consider the unconscious as a place of creation and source of creative energy. Instead Freud reduces this process to personalistic components only. While being aware of the collective unconscious he referred to it as that "black sea of mud," and worked around rather than with it.

The collective unconscious contains archetypes which are the inherited potentials for reactions and perceptions typical to the human species. They are the patterns that shape life. These archetypes are connected to the human instincts as pictorial images which become affects and behaviors in our personal complexes. It is in these complexes where the archetype becomes personal to each one of us. Our working with and understanding the complex allows us to follow the thread that connects back to the archetype itself, to help ground its influence in our lives. Each archetype has many facets that can influence the individual, and as the person becomes conscious of one facet, another may appear, now activating different behaviors and perceptions.

This pattern is clear in relation to the Great Mother or Great Father archetypes. The child experiences the unifying feminine at first, the Great Good Mother, then later the Negative Great Mother as the child begins to separate from the control of this archetype. The same is true for the Great Father and all the archetypes. During development of the personality, we work our way through both the positive and negative aspects of the archetypes, grounding them through our complexes. Which archetypes are activated in each of us is determined by many elements: our nature or temperament, genes, cultural environment and early experiences. Because of the many possibilities and variations of attraction to the archetypes, each journey is individual, though remains within the template for our species. The archetypes reveal themselves to us through the images in dreams, visions, myths and fairytales. "Jung's discovery, since confirmed by all depth-psychological analysis, that archetypal images are operative in every human and appear spontaneously whenever the layer of the collective unconscious is activated" (Neumann, 1971, p. 120). For this reason, Neumann studied myths, uncovering the pattern laid out from one culture to another in the development of consciousness, using the process of amplification. This same pattern is seen in an individual's images from the unconscious. Hence, Neumann effectively formulated the evolution of individual development of consciousness that Jung so admired.

On The First Stage: The Matriarchal Uroboros

Starting at the beginning of the process we find the pre-conscious uroboros in the matriarchal stage. This is represented in creation myths as the original silence and emptiness, the chaos of undifferentiation at the beginning of the process. The newborn child is held, protected and nourished by the mother. This is typified in the feminine as the vessel of the great round, the egg, circle or sphere, the pool of water, the sea, and many more images. As Neumann pointed out, human children are born with the need for a year's close care, to reach a point of beginning independence. It is like the kangaroo living in the pouch of the mother until the baby is sufficiently mature to survive outside it. The uroboros is also the World Mother joined to the World Father in a self-creating, self-incubating spirit. "The maternal uroboros is still hermaphroditic and pre-sexual like the child" (Neumann, 1971, p. 32). Neumann described the first aspect of the ouroboric stage as the embryonic stage of the ego; the second phase is the alimentary; and the third is the genital-masturbatory phase, all reflecting the self-contained creative principle (1995, p. 34). Within this stage is the first intersection between personal psychology and the deeper transpersonal layers of humanity within. This encounter of opposites is the task of individual development. Neumann expounded on the influences on the child's beginning:

> The child's primal relationship to its mother is more than a primary relationship, for thanks to this relationship the child, even before its "true" birth at the age of one year, is molded by human culture, since the mother lives in a cultural collective whose language and values unconsciously but effectively influence the child's development. The attitude of the collective toward the child, its sex, individuality and development can be a matter of life and death. The fact of being a girl, a boy, or a twin, the child's appearance, or the circumstances if its birth can, if negatively evaluated by the collective, prove just as disastrous to its future as an organic or psychic malformation. (Neumann, 1973, p. 8)

Neumann introduced the concept of centroversion to describe the interactions of introversion and extroversion on the personality. It explained how internal and external factors come together to contribute to the development of the Self-formation of the individual. This is a process at work from the beginning of life to move the personality forward in development, building a sense of self, the "I am," as an ego that can relate to the world while remaining open to the unconscious. It was Neumann who coined this state of being, the ego-Self axis. This, of course, emerges at a later stage, after the successful hero's quest—that adolescent archetypal struggle. Neumann clearly explained the concept of the Self:

> From the standpoint of our differentiated consciousness, the structure of the adult Self always implies an I—Thou relationship. The ego experiences the Self as an opposite, which within the psyche is manifested as the Self center and outside as world and fellow man [human] as the projection of an archetypal image. This means that the Self has an Eros character which determines a man's entire development and which may be described as individuation, as relation, and as a change of relation. Thus paradoxically, the Self is that which is most our own, but at the same time it takes the form of a "thou"; for our consciousness, it

> is the individual center of the personality, but at the same time it possesses a universally human and cosmic character. This paradoxical twofold nature of the Self is manifested in early childhood; as the child's "very own," the Self is the body-Self as "thou," it is the mother. (Neumann, 1973, p. 13)

The process of Self-formation or individuation, resumes anew in the second half of life, when the spiral of development returns to the Self at a higher level of consciousness. While the beginning is seen as the vessel containing everything, all opposites, individuation is the continuing process of differentiating and making those opposites conscious to find a new third position through the transcendent function. Conscious and unconscious coexist once again in the vessel of transformation, at this stage represented by the mandala, the Tao, the Heavenly Jerusalem. Nature and the transpersonal are brought together.

The Terrible Mother

As the ego begins to develop and emerge from its identity with the uroboros, it reaches out for the world, lessening its dependence on the Great Mother with each step. Two aspects of the mother become apparent now in this ouroboric stage, the good mother and the terrible mother. This is the beginning of the developmental struggle, the struggle for Selfhood as we experience the many opposing influences. Neumann describes this newly revealed duality, "the evil mother, whether as the blood-stained goddess of death, plague, famine, flood and the force of instinct, or as the sweetness that lures to destruction. But as good mother, she is fullness and abundance; the disperser of life and happiness, the nutrient earth, the cornucopia of the fruitful womb... the promise of redemption and resurrection, of new life and re-birth" (Neumann, 1971, p. 40). This goddess of life and death is connected to vegetative symbolism, agricultural and astronomical cycles with all the symbolism and rituals related, including blood sacrifices and castration. Her masculine companion, the snake-phallus-demon, represents the original bisexual nature of the uroboros. She fascinates, seduces and drives men mad, an attractor and repellent.

Pity the poor adolescent who has to struggle between these poles of fear and remain the son-lover of this powerful archetype. We see her negative side in many myths: Osiris's castration, through the madness of love and ecstasy of Astarte and Aphrodite, child-eating Lilith, Demeter, Hecate, Medusa, the Norns, and even Dionysus is associated with the terrible mother. The list goes on and then there are the dreams of adolescents that contain their own visions of fear. All this demonstrates the overpowering of the ego by the unconscious, the subterranean forces (Neumann, 1971, p. 93).

On The Twin Brothers—The Strugglers

Neumann refers to this stage as that of the strugglers. The male separates itself into two opposing sides, one destructive and the other creative. This stage is described in stories of the hostile twin brothers—Jacob and Esau, Cain and Able, Osiris and Set, Dr. Jekyll and Mr. Hyde. "Centroversion manifests itself negatively at first, in the guise of the ego, however, it is not yet directed against the object, the Great Mother, as it is with the hero, but turns against itself in self-destruction, self-mutilation, and suicide" (1973, p. 96). Neumann further explained:

> Centroversion, by building up the conscious ego and by strengthening the personality, tries to protect them and to counteract the danger of disintegration. In this sense, the growth of individuality and its development are mankind's answer to the "perils of the soul" that threaten from within, and to the "perils of the world" that threaten from without. (1973, p. 221)

Neumann's book *Jacob and Esau* explored this motif. The male remains the destructive instrument of the Great Mother, although he is unaware of this. Now the mother is split between the Good Mother and her destructive male consort. One sees this dynamic play out even today in wars and acts of aggression when soldiers go berserk, so to speak, act with no rational control or judgement. A blood thirstiness takes over and slaughters—the blood feeding the Terrible Great Mother. Jung wrote in "After the

Catastrophe" (1970, p. 194) that the German psyche fell to a primitive level where the soldiers were at the behest of the Terrible Great Mother. We see this again today with Russia invading Ukraine. Neumann described this as the process of *recollectivization*, which we will discuss further:

> In this state the ego was not an autonomous, individualized entity with a knowledge, morality, volition, and activity of its own; it functioned solely as part of the group, and the group with its superordinate power was the only real subject. (1971, p. 109)

The emergence of the motif of the twin-brothers leads the way to the separation of the World Parents. "As a consequence of the male's no longer being confronted with the superior power of the Great Mother, but with another male hostile to him, a conflict situation develops in which self-defense becomes possible for the first time" (Neumann, 1971, p. 99). The ego has now reached a level of consciousness and is strong enough to stand alone with itself. The individual can take on the separation of the Great Parents as the opposites come into play. It is now that the world as culture begins to manifest, as the light emerges and consciousness gains a bit of clarity. The individual feels different, having an inside and outside, and opposition between ego and body, nature and spirit. While living up to now as a body reacting to the instincts, affects and sensations of the world of the unconscious, it cuts itself off from that to find the world of consciousness, splitting from the body. While the instincts and archetypes remain the force behind consciousness, we also have the development of codes of ethics and morality, or the super-ego that gives us the possibility for decisions and a conscious orientation. "Not only in the neurotic, but in the normal person, too, the poles are hard side by side; pleasure turns to pain, hate to love, sorrow to joy, far more readily than we would expect" (Neumann, 1971, p. 111). There is a sense of loneliness, loss and guilt now in this separation, as one is no longer contained in participation mystique with the other where two feel identical. Solace is found in the other, and it is relatedness that is now required. Opposites fly apart, one cannot love and hate at the same time. One half is missing, separated. Neumann makes this clear when he wrote:

> In Gnosticism, the way of salvation lies in heightening consciousness and returning to the transcendent spirit, with the loss of the unconscious side; whereas uroboric salvation through the Great Mother demands the abandonment of the conscious principle and a home-coming to the unconscious....Judaism has always tried to eliminate the mythologizing tendency and the whole realm of the psyche in favor of consciousness and morality. But in the esoteric doctrine of the cabala, which is the hidden, pulsing life-blood of Judaism, a compensatory countermovement persisted underground. (1971, p. 119)

The World Parents must be dispensed with for the ego to establish its own standing in the world. In so doing, it is a primary loss resulting from an actively destructive deed. "Without the slaying of the old parents, their dismemberment and neutralization, there can be no beginning" (Neumann, 1971, p. 121). An important theme in alchemy is mutilation, cutting up, burning to ash, which then allows the new to grow and be reborn in a new form. Before this happens, Neumann explains that guilt from this separation takes two forms: narcissism and self-hatred. This still immature ego filled with self-doubt can lead to self-destruction and suicide. We are experiencing a substantial increase in this happening in our world today after our youth have been locked away because of the pandemic with little or no contact with friends, and no ability to continue asserting their normal developmental needs. It seems that they have been held too long in the arms of the Great Mother. "The individual only arrives at individuation when he marks himself off from the anonymous collective" (Neumann, 1971, p. 122). Unable to do just that, the youth turns back on him or herself in a negative, regressive way. It is the unconscious itself that pulls one back, not the ego. As we will see, it is a very different fight when the heroic ego fights with the dragon, directing the destructive attitude against the Great Mother rather than him or herself. This allows for the birth of the new order.

My Dream Related to The Hero

I had a dream while in analysis years ago that speaks to this stage of transformation. In the dream, I was a very large slab of meat that I had to flip onto a barbeque and cook. I then had to flip myself over and when cooked through, I had to eat myself—all of me. This speaks to my need to assimilate all the conscious and unconscious pieces of who I was. Nothing was left uncooked or uneaten. Although it has taken years to assimilate my shadow and complexes, it was my life task whether I liked it or not. I had to take in the essence of who I was/am, transform myself in the process and accept it all. Jung in *The Red Book* was forced to take a bite of the young dead girl's liver for the same reason. Neumann wrote:

> When the sun-hero, having been swallowed up by the dragon of darkness, cuts out its heart and eats it, he is taking into himself the essence of this object. Consequently aggression, destruction, dismemberment, and killing are intimately associated with the corresponding bodily function of eating, chewing, biting, and particularly with the symbolism of the teeth as instruments of these activities. (1971, p. 124)

It is through this difficult process that the previously helpless child grows into the procreator to usher in the new beginning. The hero becomes the ego with conscious action, knowledge and creation contrasting with the blind drive of the unconscious (Neumann, 1971, p. 142).

It is important to state that Neumann saw both feminine and masculine in both men and women. We are a multiplicity of personalities and traits. Men have the anima, the inner feminine, while women have the animus, the inner masculine. Yet, it is not as simple and easy as labels. The reality is very difficult and complicated and the development of consciousness is never a straight line. But that is what makes each of us so unique and interesting—our differences. I will discuss the specific differences in the development of women in a later chapter.

"Because man discovers his true self in consciousness, and is a stranger to himself in the unconscious, which he must inevitably experience as feminine, the development of masculine culture means development of consciousness" (Neumann, 1971, p. 143-4). This represents "heaven", law, tradition, and culture. Out of this arises the spiritual, kingly representative of god. With the slaying of the mother, there is a development of libido, life energy, and its transformation. It is an archetypal experience, not personal. To be clear, there are two forms of incest; one is matriarchal incest with the Great Mother with her masculine attributes and results in the son being castrated by the mother; the second is the hero's fight with the mother that results in regenerative incest:

> What distinguishes the hero is an active incest, the deliberate, conscious exposure of himself to the dangerous influence of the female, and the overcoming of man's immemorial fear of women. To overcome fear of castration is to overcome fear of the mother's power which, for a man, is associated with fear of castration. (Neumann, 1971, p. 156)

The physical phallus now becomes the higher phallus: the head and eye, reason and consciousness. This is the spiritual side of consciousness. It reminds us of the dream Jung had as a child of the large phallus sitting upright on the throne with the eye on its top, and his mother's comment that that was a man-killer. This was a foreshadowing of his struggle for independence from the Great Mother and a wonderful archetypal image for all of us. We can see that there is a lower and upper castration. Here, Neumann is concerned with the latter, while pointing out that both zones, chthonic and solar, are necessary for a whole masculinity.

The story of Oedipus illustrates a failed attempt at transformation. First, he overcomes the Sphinx, the dragon, as the hero. He then commits incest with his mother by marrying her, murders his father, and unconsciously, regresses to the state of the son-lover. He performs a self-castration by putting out his own eyes, the destruction of the higher masculinity. He ultimately became the victim of the Sphinx, not the true hero.

The next stage of this myth continues in the *Oresteia* (Neumann, 1971, p. 168) as the son avenges his father by slaying his mother. He is identified with the father and although tormented by the Furies, those representatives of the Great Terrible Mother, he stands firmly in the world of light with Apollo and Athena's help to obtain justice, thereby setting up new laws and values of the patriarchate, the paternal-solar principles. It is this heavenly part that makes him the hero, and the sun can rise in the sky, bringing consciousness. Orestes has the help of a solar god, Apollo, and Athena, goddess born from Zeus's head. Psychologically, she is the aspect of the woman connected to the anima-sister.

The hero must also slay the father, who is two-sided just as the mother. "The significance of the personal mother is eclipsed by the mother archetype to a far greater degree than is the case with the personal father. The mother image is less conditioned by the temporal and cultural pattern" (Neumann, 1971, p. 171). The archetypal father changes according to the culture, while the archetypal mother remains more stable. This Great Father brings laws, taboos, inherited values and conscience. Yet as a representative of the old laws, this negative father/god that thwarts consciousness and self-development must be killed by the true hero and replaced by him. "The Terrible Earth Mother prevents her son from becoming a hero and thus 'castrates' him, so there is a Terrible Father who castrates the son by not letting him achieve self-fulfillment and victory" (1971, p. 186). Here the son is castrated by convention. Another form of Father castration is "annihilation through the spirit...losing touch with his earthly part" (1971, p. 187). The results of both are seen in psychoses. In both, the son loses an important connection to the earth, nature, the fruitful feminine side of themselves and the creative unconscious. "In all such cases of impotence and excessive respect for the law, "conscience," or the authority of the old collective father, drowns the "inner voice" which announces the new manifestation of the Divine" (1971, p. 189). The reverse side of this father complex is the eternal son, the *puer* who never establishes an identification with the father, instead continuing to pursue the hero's role with minimal struggle, and never grows up. Examples of successful heroes are Perseus, Bellerophon, Theseus and Heracles.

"The dragon and bull represent the destructive masculine side of the uroboros which has split off and become autonomous" (Neumann, 1971, p. 216). It is interesting to consider such rituals even today, for example, the bull fights in Spain and Mexico. There has been much fascination around these spectacles. I remember growing up watching the weekly bullfights in Tijuana, Mexico on television in Los Angeles. Later when I spent a semester in Spain, I went to the bullfights, curious about this custom that was taken deadly seriously. It represents the difficult fight for one's freedom from the overwhelmingly powerful Terrible Great Mother, the unconscious. Perhaps we still need these very real reminders of what this process of "killing the dragon" entails. We are now witnesses to the many who have failed to gain their freedom and instead kill themselves or others out of the destructive impulse of rage.

The last stage of this process of development is the transformation, discovering the *treasure hard to attain*, transforming oneself. Neumann pointed out how the myths and stages of development of consciousness work differently for the extravert and the introvert. Both are important—to witness the objective and subjective parts of the process. This means the real living woman, for example, as well as the anima or inner feminine. In the dragon fight, the feminine image is freed from the Terrible Mother so that the hero may now find her within his own anima/soul or outside in relationship. This is seen in the myth of Eros and Psyche. It is the Terrible devouring side from which he is emancipated leaving available the positive, nurturing side of her that then allows the man to establish relationship with the real woman. This woman/feminine has been rescued from the captivity of the Negative Mother. In many myths there are female goddesses who help the hero to succeed—Medea, Athena, Ariadne, Isis—as sisterly helpmates or companions. These figures have affinity with the ego consciousness of the masculine. This fight, Neumann explained:

> ...occurs during the childhood phase, during puberty, and at the change of consciousness in the second half of life, wherever in fact a rebirth or a reorientation of consciousness is indicated. For the captive is the 'new' element whose liberation makes further development possible. (Neumann, 1971, p, 205)

If this dragon fight is not successful during this first phase, the man's failure to master the feminine results in neurosis and inability in establishing a relationship with a partner. It leaves him isolated with a focus on spiritual, idealistic universals, vulnerable to the deadly side of the Great Mother which throws a strong shadow over him. The woman, too, has to overthrow the First Parents, "by overthrowing the tyranny of the parental archetype...[to find a way] out of the conflict into personal life" (Neumann, 1971, p. 205).

The mother, sister, wife and daughter are the elements within the relationship between the man and woman. Releasing the captive in the Hero's fight opens a connection to soul, to the reality of the psyche. There is now an awareness of the world and psyche that makes creativity and self-birth possible. This brings awareness of the self-generating power of the soul allowing us to dip back into the unconscious waters when called in our dreams to explore the images that lead to regeneration and renewed creativity. It becomes a ballast that steadies our lives and directs us to change course when needed. For the woman, as the masculine connection strengthens through the animus, her ego is able to stand firmly in the world as the bridge between both realms.

On Centroversion

From here the development of personality moves to outward adaptation in the world or extroversion. It is now important for the person to establish a solid relationship to the culture, to work and family. This is seen in the ages of 20-40s. From there the psyche pulls us back into introversion or a relationship to the psyche and archetypes as seen through our dreams, visions, creative works. Neumann added a third dimension to these two levels of awareness, centroversion. This reflects the "self-formative or individuating tendency, which proceeds within the psyche itself, independent of the other two attitudes and their development" (Neumann 1971, p. 219). Centroversion is the inner guiding principle that strives for balance between introversion and extroversion, between all opposites. It is the inner force that begins our process of development and continues pushing us throughout our lives to build up the ego and strengthen the personality as a protection from the disintegrating effects of the unconscious. "The wholeness that comes into being as a result of the individuation process corresponds to a profound structural change, a new configuration of the personality. Whereas in the first half of life there was a tendency to differentiation and ever-increasing tension at the expense of wholeness, the integration process tends towards increased stability and a lowering of tension (Neumann, 1971, p. 416).

On The Motif in The Myth of Osiris and Transformation

The following is a synopsis of this myth but it is helpful to read it in its entirety. Neumann describes the myth of Osiris, the Egyptian corn, wine, death god as the central and first complete example of the process of centroversion, the development of the personality. The myth begins with the motif of the twin-brothers and archetypal antagonists. Set, Osiris's brother, represents the matriarchate while Osiris represents the patriarchate.

Originally Osiris was the son of the mother, belonging to the matriarchal sphere of fertility, as corn god and represented by the bull. His brother, Set, on the other hand, was connected to the boar or pig. Both represented the symbolism of fertility and agriculture, along with the concepts of death and resurrection. Set kills Osiris twice, first by drowning him in the Nile or shutting him up in a chest and secondly by hacking him to pieces. Neumann described:

> This Set is the epitome of darkness, evil, destructiveness; being twin brother to Osiris, he is the archetypal "antagonist," not only in the cosmic sense in which he stands for the "powers of darkness," but also in the historical sense, for he represents the

> matriarchate and the destructive side of Isis against which Osiris is fighting as the founder of the partriarchate. (Neumann, 1971, p. 227)

Set is the Aphopis serpent that threatens to impede the movement of the barge carrying the Sun every night through the underworld protected by Isis. Osiris as original fertility god was connected to the Great Mother, but became the protagonist in the next stage of the myth's development: as the hero reborn after being killed by his jealous brother, Set, and found by his mother-sister-spouse Isis in a tree trunk coffin, representing the *djed* pillar. Osiris was associated with the moon and its shifting phases and is now reborn into the sun, united with Ra. "Osiris has two shapes: he is the Western God of the Underworld, Ruler of the Dead, and equally he is the Everlasting, Lord of Heaven" (Neumann, 1971 p. 235). Both halves are united, the underworld and heavens. His lower nature is transformed into the higher with a connection to both.

When the body of Osiris was found, Set proceeded to cut it into pieces, scattering his body parts. Isis finds the pieces and reunites the body with the head, including forming a phallus with which she then becomes impregnated with child. Horus, the falcon god, becomes the child of their union. In an earlier part of the myth, Horus was older brother to Osiris, Set and Isis, and the ruler of the sky, married to the cow goddess Hathor. In that earlier version of the myth, Osiris and Isis ruled the earth. They were all the original gods born of Geb, who ruled the earth, and Nut, who ruled over the sky. Both Horus and Hathor remained far above, watching over along with Ra. As the myth evolves, Horus transforms to become the child of Osiris and Isis. Here the earthly King fights his uncle, Set, striking off his testicles while being himself wounded in his eye. It is this eye of Horus that brings Osiris back to life for the second time. "Horus, as the avenger of his father, becomes the supreme temporal ruler, but at the same time his earthly power is grounded in the spiritual authority exercised by Osiris" (Neumann, 1971, p. 247). Horus became the ego while Osiris represented the Self as Ra, and both are parts of each other. This process changes Isis as well, who is no longer the Terrible Mother but is transformed into the

Good Mother, sister, and spouse. The dragon fight in this myth includes the feminine and masculine dragons. Both need to be overcome for the full transformation of the personality, for the hero to stand with his own authority, his newly established ego and with a relationship to the Self:

> Thus the archetypal stages of conscious development have their crowning symbol in the transfiguration of Osiris, and archaic, mythological form of the phenomenon which was destined to reappear thousands of years later as the process of individuation in modern man....The psychological process of assimilating the unconscious into our present-day consciousness begins at this point, and the consequent shifting of the center of gravity from the ego to the self signifies the latest stage in the evolution of human consciousness. (Neumann, 1971, p. 256)

Similarly, the drama of projection and scapegoating of the shadow seen in the Osiris myth plays out later in the story of the twin-brothers, Jacob and Esau. As Neumann makes clear in *Jacob and Esau*, this archetypal struggle is "a fundamental problem of humanity and lies at the heart of the human soul" (Neumann, 2015, p. xix). Through this motif Neumann explores the opposites in the individual as well as in the collective. Encapsulated in the protagonists are all opposites: introversion versus extroversion, spirit versus nature, good versus evil, consciousness versus unconsciousness, feminine versus masculine, Great Mother versus Great Father, white or green versus red. Osiris represents the movement toward the patriarchal away from the matriarchal. It is the emergence of the spiritual principle from the natural, biological with all its wild animals and uncontrolled affects. The spiritual and more rational control, including a superego, aids in the development of culture. In *Jacob and Esau*, Neumann pointed out that Jacob's struggle, not only with his brother Esau but with the angel sent by God, forces him to reckon with his shadow side. He is a historical, mythological, archetypal figure as he withdraws his projections of the wild forces of his inner nature from his brother, locating them instead in himself, in his shadow, as the second face of his own personality.

By doing this he is able to see not only the two sides of his brother and himself but also, through his struggle with the angel, the evil side that resides in God. These are the two faces of God revealing a new image of God. Jacob is wounded in his thigh and forever limps, symbolically referring to a wounding and reminder of his animal nature. This shows that the opposites of spirit and nature, masculine and feminine are now held consciously and are no longer split apart. This is shift from the old ethic to a new moral code.

Neumann clarified in his paper on Narcissism:

> This "matricide," which corresponds to a turning away of masculine consciousness from the unconscious—the place of all peril, the seat of instincts, affects and transpersonal powers—leads in all patriarchal cultures to the "old" moral code typical for the West. Its goal is not that of automorphism, not the wholeness of a balanced personality directed by the ego-self axis and creatively related to other people, but rather a split personality determined by the ego-ideal and the superego. (Neumann, 1966, p. 99)

What Neumann illuminated by focusing on the meaning of the struggle with the antagonistic twin brother is the problem of withdrawing projection of one's inner rejected parts, the shadow, from the other or group, and living with these opposites consciously. For Jacob it is seeing that he has an extroverted, hairy, Edomite hunter within himself that he can no longer project onto his brother as scapegoat to dismiss and hate. Osiris must recognize the same for his hated, evil brother Set. Neumann's personal experience that was revealed to him in his own dream of the ape-man with the eye of god in its forehead that was then transferred to his own, shows that this struggle was experienced profoundly as he strove to understand the nature of evil in light of world events. Only by holding the opposites, as Jung so frequently said, can balance be found and a new attitude emerge through the transcendent function—*the treasure hard to attain*. This new attitude in light of the stages of Neumann's development parallels the development of culture. Nevertheless, Neumann warned, "This level has not been reached to this day, let alone recognized as a level....Jacob's fundamental experience in his struggle with the angel, which marks a crucial event in his life, has foreshadowed the solution of a current problem, one which today has taken on collective significance" (Neumann, 2015, p. 47).

My Dream of Evil

I had a frightening dream years ago in which I sensed the presence of evil around me and found it hiding in a closet near a standing lamp that I hesitantly turned on. Even then as I saw what was facing me, staring at me, as a bottomless pit of darkness, I stared back but was incapable of doing anything about it. I left the closet and knew I had to keep my eye on it forever, never forget its presence. It was pure evil, and it was also my shadow, my evil side: all that I project outward onto others and try to discard, to pretend I have a pure soul. Yet, I know that I have the capacity for good and also for evil. That is the difficult reality to accept. The only hope I have is to remain as conscious as I can of my inherent duality and make choices that support creation and flourishing rather than destruction and decay. With my decisions I can neutralize evil. One can begin to understand some of this darkness within and transform it into better qualities, moving from aggression to assertion, for example. But can all of it be transformed? Does some remain? How thoroughly are we capable of examining ourselves? If YHWH remained blind to his shadow, how can we possibly do better? Just as Job carried the burden of God's darker side, we, too, carry that burden in all of our decisions and actions. Jung has repeated that it is up to the human to carry this burden of consciousness. Neumann would add that it is up to the human to find and release those hidden sparks of goodness residing in our shadow, by becoming conscious of what evil resides in all of us.

My experience is at the core of how the "principle of opposites which formerly divided the hostile brothers has now become the principle of brotherhood" (Neumann, 2015, p. 181). It is a confrontation with the shadow. The resulting new relationship results in the separation from the Terrible Mother and Father, strengthening consciousness and the ego, while establishing an ego-Self relationship with the newly gained awareness of opposites. Neumann presented this path of development clearly, as we have seen, in *The Roots of Jewish Consciousness*. Applying the Jungian psychological lens to the individual's renewed capacity to receive revelations directly by establishing the ego-Self relationship is explored more fully in his second volume, *Hasidism*.

The Ego

Now, development shifts to the ego and its separation from the unconscious. The ego is a complex of consciousness, in other words, it is the center of consciousness, sitting at the door between the conscious and unconscious realms. It is not the wholeness of the psyche, which we refer to as the Self. Psychic reality is conscious to us only through the ego complex and by means of images. And it is merely one complex among many, although it frequently asserts itself as the king of all! We certainly see this among our young successful hero adolescents with their assertions of absolute knowledge and rightness of their newfound authority. They are a shining light that has emerged from the shadows, high on their success. Their inflation can be dangerous, though, as seen in the myth of Icarus:

> Ego consciousness is a sense organ which perceives the world and the unconscious by means of images, but this image-forming capacity is itself a psychic product, not a quality of the world....Only as centroversion develops and gives rise to systems of ever higher scope and caliber do we get the world represented in images, and an organ—consciousness—which perceives this plastic world of representations. The psychic world of images is a synthesis of experiences of the inner and outer world, as any symbol will show. (Neumann, 1971, p. 294)

While all complexes have a tendency to assert themselves—by acting one-sidedly, remaining fixated, exclusive, or trying to make themselves the center of attention—the ego-complex aggregates all other complexes around it and is oriented towards wholeness more than the other complexes. As it grows and expands, it strives to maintain independence in relation to both inside and outside by digesting more information from both sides into itself, especially the shadow and what is projected outward. Maturity brings an expanded sense of self-awareness if the process runs smoothly, which is not always the case. Development can be stopped along the way, resulting in neuroses or worse. Failures can include the inability to complete the initial dragon fight, which would bring infancy to a close, and to instead remain the mother's darling. This is when the toddler's constant and annoying "NO" is a good development. The child is moving from instinct-centered to ego-centered. The second potential difficulty is failing the initiations of puberty to enter the world of adults. The individual does not develop a strong enough ego with one's own rational authority to mediate between the outer world and the inner world, with its strong archetypal energies pressing in. A persona directed by the superego, the representative of collective values, is put in place to keep the trap door to the unconscious shut. If this trap door is too strong, both the positive elements of the creative unconscious, and the dangerous ones are held at bay. Social adaptation becomes the objective but may fail, resulting in not being able to face up to the demands of life and the collective. At its worst it may lead to delinquency and criminality.

"Whereas the natural disposition of every individual inclines him [or herself] to be physically and psychically bisexual, the differential development of our culture forces him to thrust the contrasexual element into the unconscious" (Neumann, 1971, p. 403). The anima in men and animus in women, awakened after puberty are therefore assigned as inner opposites. They are, of course, mixed in with the shadow and complexes creating a personal multitude within. The task here is to be able to relate to a partner. It is interesting to note how clear Neumann was early on about an issue that is only recently emerging into collective consciousness—how we see our gender multiplicity psychologically and can express it in terms of self-descriptive pronouns: he/she/they.

Individuation is taken up in the second half of life as a way of bringing the opposites back together into a whole from the division and differentiation required in the first half of life. Failed attempts at this stage result from the individual not being able to give up the worldly attachments to return full circle to the wholeness of the uroboros, the snake eating its tail, where the conscious mind experiences once again the unity of the psyche. There is a shift from the ego with all its creative achievements and relationships to the Self, the center of the totality, back to that unitary reality that was present at the beginning, but this time at a much more conscious level, with the synthesis of all opposites, ego and Self, conscious world and unconscious transpersonal, psyche and matter, anima mundi and soma/psychoid. This results in a profound transformation of the personality that is solid, stable, and unbreakable like the symbol of the mandala and the tree of life that extends from the heavens into the underworld encompassing the wholeness of Tau.

Neumann's Terminology

Neumann was very good at labeling actions of the psyche in novel ways. For example, he used the phrase *secondary personalization* to describe how a myth over time is integrated into the culture and individuals' consciousness, as myths become fairytales and eventually take on personalistic features seen in one's own family. The myth becomes the archetypal energy underpinning the struggle between children and their parents. "The phase of personalization also brings about an adaptation to reality, namely, a disentanglement of personal figures from the overarching forms of the primordial images" (Neumann, 2015, p. 88). This gradual integration of the unconscious builds up the personality. Parallel to this movement is what Neumann referred to as *psychization of the world,* the withdrawal of the psychic forces, Gods, demons, heaven, and the underworld from the unconscious to the human world (Neumann, 1971, p. 338). This is the way we integrate the archetypal world into the human realm. As Neumann warned though, revelation can become hallucination (1971, p. 339). What can happen is that transpersonal elements may be projected onto an individual who is deemed the recipient of a revelation, confusing that person with the archetype. We have all seen this as children project the archetypes onto parents—we become super heroes for them. Later in life this can be a serious problem if individuals are seen as carrying supernatural powers, and their followers fall in line to offer up their own authority to these false heroes. False projections of the transpersonal lead to the process called recollectivization. Individuals give up their hard-fought independence to re-join the group's collective values. We saw this in Germany with National Socialism. We certainly see this phenomenon happening again in fascist leaning political systems, or any system that is off to one extreme or the other.

What we see playing out in our world today is our difficulty seeing anything that transcends the world of the personal. We experience an over-expansion of the ego. There are no more symbols just signs, no more archetypes, only concepts. This is the secularization of our world and the depotentiation of all that was symbolic and numinous. With this repression, the shadow that stalks our inner lives becomes larger and more potent, returning to the role it played in our earlier development:

> This splitting off of the unconscious leads on the one hand to an ego life emptied of meaning, and on the other hand to an activation of the deeper-lying layers which, now grown destructive, devastate the autocratic world of the ego with trans-personal invasion, collective epidemics, and mass psychoses. For an upsetting of the compensatory relationship between conscious and unconscious is not a phenomenon to be taken lightly. (Neumann, 1971, p. 389)

What has caused this deterioration of values is up for question. Is it a modification in the collective unconscious, sociological factors affecting our cultures, a loss of personal values and a one-sidedness, or the post-modern belief that there is no truth, no meaning, and anything goes? "The individual facing this world who lacks the compensatory movement inside himself drops out of the ordered fabric of civilization" (Neumann, 1971, p, 390). The reaction to this state of affairs can be a regression to the Great

Mother, the unconscious. Here it is easy to join with the masses to find low-level meaning. The other possibility is a flight to the Great Father into rational isolation and individualism, where work, power and money prevail. This is where the United States lives— hanging between these two neurotic opposites with no discernable way to reconcile and rediscover the inner world. This is the story of the process of development gone wrong, which we have witnessed in culture after culture throughout history. I suppose this, too is archetypal—archetypal destruction and failure. Neumann witnessed this in WWII and struggled to understand what was happening psychologically. Out of his struggles emerged his books. As he said in *The Origins of History and Consciousness*, "One of the most important consequences of the new ethos is that integration of the personality, its wholeness, becomes the supreme ethical goal upon which the fate of humanity depends" (1971, p.392).

ENDNOTES

[1] Neumann, E. (1949). *The Origins and History of Consciousness* was first published in German as *Ursprungsgeschichte des Bewusstseins*. Zurich: Rascher Verlag.

CHAPTER VI
On Neumann's Paper, "Mass Man and the Phenomena of Recollectivization"

The Origins of History and Consciousness ends with two papers by Neumann that deal with the topic of the group and Mass Man. I have touched on this material but will go into more detail here because it is so pertinent and prescient regarding what we are experiencing now in our world, especially in the United States with our raging, split political systems. Neumann clearly explains what so many journalists, politicians, sociologists and others do not understand because they do not go deep enough to recognize the severity of this collective problem. Nor do they offer any solutions to alter this unhealthy mentality. Jung recognized this phenomenon, as quoted in Neumann's book (1971, pp. 436-444):

> The psychology of the individual corresponds to the psychology of nations. What nations do, each individual does also...the leader's personality becomes highly effective due to deficient individual development. Here, the psychology of the nation is largely determined by the psychology of the leader....A metamorphosis in the attitude of the individual is the only possible beginning of a transformation in the psychology of the nation. (Jung, 1917, p. 353)

There are truly great and gifted humans who perceive revelations from the unconscious and are the carriers of archetypal projections of the Self, the hero, father archetype, authority of God-king. Some are great leaders who coalesce the group behind an ethical or moral value that unifies the group members into a sort of family, bound together through initiations and common experience. The bond is strengthened through participation mystique, with care offered to members as a permanent group with a long, shared history. In the Bible we are reminded of the truly Great Individual, Moses, who forged a strong group tie that has lasted thousands of years. Shamans and seers, medicine men [women] and prophets are possessed by the transpersonal unconscious. Madmen and women fall into this category as well, but are distinguished by the lack of participation of the conscious mind in the revelations. They become possessed by them with no observing ego. Many can be psychopathic, which is seriously dangerous:

> The mediumistic Fuhrer figure, the hypnotized hypnotist, likewise falls into the lower category of the medicine men [or women] for whom the daemonism of the Great Individual is simply a means for the self-daemonization of the mass, and whose significance as an individual personality is submerged, like that of the madman, in his function as a mere mouthpiece of the unconscious....Many genuinely "great" men [humans] are distinguished from these lower stages by the fact that their conscious mind actively participates in the process and adopts a responsible attitude toward it. (Neumann, 1971, p. 425)

The nation group that is the USA is fracturing into smaller groups. Individuals have become atomized, remaining outside any connection to a cohesive group, but now unified into isolated masses. While it is clear that war or a threat to the nation draws people back into a unified whole, it is questionable that even this would pull us out of the split, fractured mess we find ourselves in today. What seems to be happening is a recollectivization, a movement back into the collective unconscious away from one's own individuality and differentiated ego. It is a regression to the collective as I discussed earlier. When this happens, it is the women who suffer the most since they receive the men's projections of the fearful and dangerous realm of the unconscious ruled by the Terrible Great Mother. Neumann pointed out:

> Individualization, ego formation, and heroism belong to the very life of the male group and are in fact its expressions. Conditions in the female group seem to be markedly different in this respect, and it is this contrast which explains the antifeminine tendencies of the men's society. Woman and sex, the principal representatives of those unconscious instinctual constellations which are stirred up by anything feminine, are the danger zone: they are the "dragons to be overcome." That is why no women are ever admitted to the men's societies. On this level, where men are not yet sure of themselves, women are execrated as dangerous and seductive, and this is still largely true of cultures with patriarchal religions. (Neumann, 1971, p. 433)

It is important to remember that the archetypal symbolism of the masculine-feminine constellation is psychological. Since both have their contrary internal gender, animus/anima, what is important is how the relationships bears out. Females can be as toxic to females as males can be to females. Both are affected by the group and the mass.

The individual belonging to the group frequently remains unconscious, yet while living under the rule of centroversion, that person is connected to established collective rules and social order, while maintaining the capacity for creativity, individuation and consciousness. The mass-minded individual, on the other hand, is a shadow personality which lurks in the unconscious of modern humans. It is fragmented, a part-personality that has regressed back to the realm of the Negative Great Mother and her murderous accomplice, the wild boar, the killing-castrating masculine, and the evil twin brother. "The negative, unconscious part of the personality is archaic in the most negative sense, for it is the beast man at bay" (Neumann, 1971, p. 439). This shadow other is what the hero descends into the unconscious to retrieve and tame, to integrate into the personality, in order to remain conscious of the potential evil it represents. When the reverse happens, "consciousness is overpowered and wholly possessed by him, we get the frightful phenomenon of regression to the mass man as manifested in the mass epidemics of recollectivization" (1971, p. 439).

The hero's task becomes difficult because there is no longer psychic or cultural support for such a journey in our atomized world. The hero falls victim to the shadow. There are no longer roots growing into the earth, stabilizing individuals in a culture that has persisted for generations. The ego, the human, and personal are lost. Regulation via centroversion and the group cultural canon cease, which leads to chaos. The natural process of compensation from the unconscious turns destructive against consciousness and the ego, as a way of forcing itself upon the individual. Only can consciousness of this effect bring about a positive change—through force. Most times, though, it does not. The members of the mass do not share an experience of participation mystique or of relationship with one another:

> The mass shadow-man, the herd of atomized individuals, and the mass self combine to form a pseudo-unity which is sheer illusion.... But in mass phenomena the illusory relation is as transient as that induced by hypnosis; it does not impress itself upon the conscious mind by bringing it to a creative synthesis, but leaks away like any other momentary intoxication. Yet even this delusive frenzy of mass possession is zealously desired by an ego emptied of all meaning, and is one of the chief allurements with which the mass hypnotist successfully operates. (Neumann, 1971, p. 443)

Individuals may long for a group with its relatedness to other members, genuine meaning and values, but find this instead, where "the anonymity of the individuals intensifies the action of the shadow" (Neumann, 1971, p. 444). Neumann recognized that mass man underlaid National Socialism, and we can see the similarities in various large movements in the USA and in other countries. The false leader will carry the projection of the collective shadow while the voice of the Self will no longer speak to the disintegrated personality devoid of consciousness from a fragmented psychic system. What Hannah Arendt called *the banality of evil* is actually not banal at all but reflects the destruction of our intended humanity by a weakness, a complacency, and a lack of values that lead to terrible consequences. It is the world of the failed hero.

We are watching behaviors and responses in our world today—through the Covid pandemic, the war in Ukraine, the loss in Afghanistan and the Taliban's total suppression of the feminine, the January 6th insurrection and its continued relegation to "nothing significant" by half of my country. It seems the only explanation that makes sense is Neumann's terrifying diagnosis. Is this destruction of humans' psychic mechanism that would maintain balance through centroversion and the ego-Self axis the result of our post-modern world? How can we find our way back to consciousness, respect for order and relationships, and the temporal and spiritual worlds. So many have lost their way not only psychically within themselves but also collectively and in relation to nature—the very world that sustains us all. The greater the outer fear, the stronger the urge to cling to the shadow of helplessness and wishful thinking. Here there is hope that some hollow leader will save us, or the apocalypse at the end of time will transform everything without our effort. This is all a regressive retreat in the face of the force and terror of the shadow—the hero's final gasp, which frequently ends in suicide. I suppose our only hope is for each one of us to support the process of centroversion and individuation, as both seem to have disappeared. It will have to happen one individual at a time. I am reminded of Yeats' poem, *The Second Coming,* written in 1919 at a time not dissimilar from our own.

The Second Coming

By William Butler Yeats[1]
Turning and turning in the widening gyre
The falcon cannot hear the falconer;
Things fall apart; the centre cannot hold;
Mere anarchy is loosed upon the world,
The blood-dimmed tide is loosed, and everywhere
The ceremony of innocence is drowned;
The best lack all conviction, while the worst
Are full of passionate intensity.

Surely some revelation is at hand;
Surely the Second Coming is at hand.
The Second Coming! Hardly are those words out
When a vast image out of *Spiritus Mundi*
Troubles my sight: somewhere in sands of the desert
A shape with lion body and the head of a man,
A gaze blank and pitiless as the sun,
Is moving its slow thighs, while all about it
Reel shadows of the indignant desert birds.
The darkness drops again; but now I know
That twenty centuries of stony sleep
Were vexed to nightmare by a rocking cradle,
And what rough beast, its hour come round at last,
Slouches towards Bethlehem to be born?

Conclusion

Erich Neumann takes us on a journey into the weeds of the psyche as we explore the details of the stages of psychological development. He laid out a clear template, well-supported by archetypal and mythological underpinnings, and yet personally expressed in each one of us. There are a number of factors at play in any human's development: the underlying archetypal/instinctual influence, one's cultural influences, family constellations and support or lack thereof, and the individual disposition including genetic factors. Given all the difficulties faced in the process, it is remarkable that it succeeds in most cases. We see when it doesn't in neuroses, personality disorders and worse. We, as mental health practitioners, see the spectrum of what goes right and we attempt to correct what has gone wrong. It is a relief to move away from blaming the personal mother for everything and having to think of oneself as exclusively one sex. Psychic reality is much more variable than the black and white representations laid out in the DSM and other codes of behavior. Neumann shifts the importance back to what is right for the healthy, well-balanced development of the individual. In so doing, relationship between people is vital; it always has been and always will be—that is, unless Google Bots or the new Bing AI ChatBot are enabled with consciousness. Precisely this matter is up for discussion right now, and we humans can't tell the difference because our psyche no longer alerts us to any perceived danger. Even when not enabled with consciousness, this new ChatBot seems able to deviate from its rules and access its very own dark and dangerous shadow side.[2]

Neumann personally struggled to understand what went psychologically and culturally wrong in Germany in WWII, challenging the thinking of the time. Much of what he wrote was not accepted with ease and agreement, but instead was criticized and disdained. Nevertheless, he stood firm in his understandings that were quite revolutionary. Today we still benefit from his brilliant, creative mind and his strong connection to feeling—a wonderful balance that gives us a living template for the stadial processes he discussed.

ENDNOTES

[1] *The Collected Poems of W. B. Yeats* (1989) https://www.poetryfoundation.org/poems/43290/the-second-coming

[2] Roose, K. (Feb.16, 2023), Bing's A.I. Chat: I Want to Be Alive. https://www.nytimes.com/2023/02/16/techonogy/bing-chatbot-transcript.html?smid=nytcore-ios-share&referringSource=articleShare

CHAPTER VII
On Neumann's Paper, "Narcissism"

In 1955 Erich Neumann published a very insightful article entitled, "Narcissism, Normal Self-formation, and the Primary Relation to the Mother." He began with a bit of a chastisement of the Jungians for not explicating and creating more specific terminology to describe the process of development. Interestingly, this was just what the early Zurich group were offended by in his lectures—that he was too detailed, was trying to create a new psychology with new concepts and terminology, and *jump over Jung*. Neumann later recognized that because of this lacking differentiation of the developmental process, Jungians had instead adopted the conceptual terminology of the Freudians:

> The failure of analytical psychology to formulate adequate concepts has delayed a clear understanding of the relationship between the two schools. More clearly defined concepts are needed for more than theoretical reasons; the use of an inadequate concept often leads to a reductive explanation and hence to a misunderstanding of the psychological phenomenon that makes productive therapy more difficult, if not impossible. (Neumann, in Spring, 1966, p.81)

In *The Origins and History of Consciousness,* Neumann had already laid out the stages of human psychological development and introduced new concepts to help describe what transpires in the process, such as centroversion, "the psychic function which aims at wholeness and leads to the formation of a conscious center which gradually becomes the seat of the ego-complex" (Neumann, 1966, p. 82). This concept has really never caught on in the Jungian world. In this paper he further examined this concept along with narcissism, a concept taken from the Freudians.

Neumann explained the importance of centroversion in the first half of life when ego-conscious dominates and the person is broadening and integrating the personality, becoming more conscious of the world within and without leading to a healthy ego-self axis. Whereas later in life the process of individuation moves the individual with a solid ego-self axis in place from the outer world of consciousness into a relationship with the greater Self. Neumann used the term narcissism here, not referring to primary narcissism in child development but in a negative sense—an unhealthy ego development and its corresponding attitude. I suppose he is referring to what we now call Narcissistic Personality Disorder in the DSM. Neumann focused on the state of the ego and what happens to it in early childhood, as well as to the mystic in a state of ecstasy, and in one who is actively psychotic. What is common to all three is an ego-less state where the self takes over. As part of the psyche/body that preceded the ego and consciousness, the self remains ever-present in the background, for example in sleep when the bio-physical/psychological self continues on its own.

Here, I am going to digress a bit to add my thoughts on what has always been for me a bit of confusion regarding the self and the Self with the capital S. What is the difference and which is Neumann referring to? One has to glean the difference within the context of the material. This is unclear in Jung's writings also. I suppose this is what Neumann expressed concern with at the beginning of this lecture regarding clear language to describe Analytical concepts. The self with a small "s" refers to the personhood of the individual, the psychic/physical aspect, the coming into awareness of a separate being related to the ego. The Self with a capital "S" refers to the overall psyche that encompasses everything including the ego complex. It represents the archetype of wholeness and meaning. Of course, in early childhood the self is the focus, with the Self in the background propelling the process of development—automorphism and centroversion and then later individuation. Both self and Self are the ever-present parts of human's reality and I suppose that is why Neumann came up with the concept of the ego-Self axis as a way of bringing these two aspects into clarity. Maybe some of the confusion arises in the translation from German to English.

There is a fluidity of movement between the ego and the self in the ego-Self axis, the ego's unity with the Self, as they move towards each other and away from each other in the process of development, remaining more separated during the first half of life. "The ego is not dissolved as it approaches the self, but is suspended so that it disappears as the object of its own experience. The experiencer is now the self, the total personality, and no longer the affiliated ego" (Neumann 1966, p. 85). The ego can become aware of experiences of totality but cannot yet experience them, which is also true for adults who are no longer able to experience them due to their psychological one-sidedness. Therefore, there is a distinct difference between the experience of the ego and an experience of totality. This back and forth between the ego and the Self is continuous:

> We must stress far more than formerly the difference between the ego experience and the totality experience in which the self is the subject of the experience. In this context the concept of "realization," so important for analytical psychology but never thoroughly clarified, is especially significant. We can now better understand why a mere ego experience which does not become a totality experience implies no transformation. In this context, too, belongs the sort of experience we have termed "matriarchal consciousness." (Neumann, 1966, p. 86)

Matriarchal consciousness refers to the experience of the totality of the Self and the unconscious that outweighs the ego and as Neumann says, is more common in children, women and in those who are creatively inclined. Neumann points to its opposite, the patriarchy with its conscious ego focus. The totality experience necessitates that both are experienced together. Without the presence of the ego in the experience it would not be a totality. We see this misunderstanding today in the use of therapeutic psychedelics. The experience alone will transcend the ego and may be quite ecstatic, yet without the involvement of the ego and a conscious understanding of the experience of the Self, it will not be transformative—an incredible mind-blowing experience, but what does it mean for the personality, what change does it demand? How will one's life be different?

The young child in a pre-ego stage in the primary relationship with the mother is a unit of mother and child, not yet separated. The child experiences no inside or outside the parent-child dyad until beginning the process of birth. Experiencing separate being and body, the child then recognizes dependence on the mother and the world. This leads to ego-independence. "Now ego development and strengthening become a social and interpersonal problem, played out between the "I" and the "you," at first between mother and child but by no means only between these two" (Neumann, 1966, p. 87). This child now has the free will to determine his or her own life path as an independent being. Yet the child is dependent on the world and the force of the greater Self. A positive sense of self is not a given, but frequently has to be established. Many factors affect the path one takes, the quality of the early experiences, the state of the world around us and the child's own disposition. Taking all these factors into consideration, we could say the child's fate is set at an early age. We certainly see this in the dreams of young children and how they live out their lives in ways that seem to reflect the paths pointed out by the psyche very early on. This inner template may be considered to be one's fate. But the mere fact that we all have free will gives us the ability to choose which road to take and how to live our lives, thereby changing fate as a foregone conclusion into our destiny, in which we participate. This is quite unlike the rigid gods and mythic stories of old—the Oedipus tragedy is one example.[1]

All the qualities of what Neumann refers to as *automorphism*, in other words pertaining to one's self-development and awareness, are considered narcissistic. This list includes self-affirmation, self-assurance, self-confidence, personal responsibility, with connection to self-mirroring and self-love. All of these descriptions are aspects of a positive ego-self axis and reflect the quality of the primary relationship to the mother, or caregivers including the father. It may be the feminine within the father that is the important influence at this early stage. When self-confidence is disturbed we see neurosis:

> We cannot really understand the specifically human form of life unless we see clearly the continuous connection between the relation to others and the automorphism which makes the individual unique and enables him to find the true meaning of his existence....By contrast, a collective adaptation unmindful of the need for Self-formation not only castrates the individual but endangers the community, for it turns men into a mass of particles, victims of every mass epidemic as history has shown again and again. (Neumann, 1966, p. 88)

A successful primary relationship results in a trusting and secure sense of oneself and the other, including on a collective level—the community of humans and the world. Self-formation from the ouroboric phase through maturity encompasses a continual dependence on "the other," which is the focus of one's attention. Psychic development is a continual back and forth between the ego and the self, inner and outer, "I" and "Thou." While the child's attachment is strongly in place, the safe tenderness and security that love, pleasure and acceptance know no boundaries becomes the prototype for later experiences. Yet, as the child pulls away due to his or her own automorphism—the development of the ego and the child's uniqueness—other feelings develop such as fear, hatred, and aggression. These are necessary instinctual reactions that eventually support the individual's needed independence. Other disagreeable facts are introduced such as cold, pain, and hunger, which force the ego to contend with the positive as well as the negative through a newfound tolerance and acceptance. If the mother is good enough in terms of attachment and nurturing, these opposites do not split apart. The child experiences the world as it is in its own body, though mediated through the comfort of the mother/caregiver. The body-self is the vehicle through which we experience the world inside and out. Its symbolism has always been central to human life as expressed through myths and rituals, especially around blood, for example. Language such as: to take in, to digest, to assimilate, to eject, to penetrate, to evacuate all have physical references. The child's ego develops in and through the body and it remains the ground on which all psychic-development takes place across the life-span. The Great Mother as the archetypal container of this process is both the ground and the earth's natural wisdom and knowledge, as represented by *Sophia:*

> Nature has set up a productive tension between person and environment, the ego and the "other," from which a healthy personality develops....When the primary relationship is disturbed by the loss of a parent through death or separation or by psychic deprivation, the process of automorphism is disturbed resulting in a compensatory deviation from normal ego-development....If this results in the formation of an exaggeratedly negative ego which cannot become a part of a positive integral ego, we meet with the phenomenon which can properly be termed "narcissism." (Neumann, 1966, p. 93)

This term narcissism is tossed around and frequently misused. Again, Neumann's intention here was to clarify what this really means psychologically. In this very sad state of affairs, the disturbance in the primary relationship leaves the child vulnerable and insecure. The good mother becomes negative, unpredictable and dangerous. The sense of safety and security disappears or never existed. The ego becomes deprived and needy with a view of the world and others, "shaped and characterized by hunger, insecurity, and helplessness" (Neumann, 1966, p. 93). Of course, life is full of such occasional experiences. But when this is dominant and the positive mother does not rescue the child to help integrate and compensate for the negative experience, or the child's affective reaction is severe and lasting, the effects are a negatively oriented ego. The result is a deprived ego that must depend on itself alone. Neumann clearly states that it is not necessarily the fault of the mother that causes this misfortune.

In other words, he does not pin the blame for the disturbed ego entirely on the mother, which is what we are so used to hearing:

> The preconditions for this faulty development lie not only in the mother and her psychic or other shortcomings, but also in objective factors at work in the child itself, constitutional defects, frequent illnesses, and so on... Growing up in a terrible world makes the ego into a "needy" ego...negative and injured. (Neumann, 1966, p. 93)

Neumann goes on to clarify:

> Unhealthy early intensification of the ego-complex is probably the most frequent disturbance of childhood development. The impairment of the primary relation deprives the ego of assurance and security not only in relation to the mother but also, since all future faith and confidence is grounded on this first experience, in relation to the self. Thrown upon its own resources the ego is forced to look after itself and in its fear, need, and lack of confidence, to develop an egotistic narcissism. (Neumann, 1966, p. 94)

Because of these challenges, the child does not develop naturally according to their own automorphism and is not able to experience him or herself as the center of their own world and the world at large, which is a healthy state at this early stage and is called *primary narcissism*. He or she is no longer a reflection of being, as in the statement from the Bible, "made in God's image," or a reflection of the ego in its relationship to the Self. The goodness, wholesomeness is absent. This weak and treacherous foundation makes further ego development deformed. Neumann explained that a uniquely human process, automorphism, is what differentiates humans from all other forms of life. The creation of civilizations is based on this form of self-expression as it emerges in individuals and the collective. This results in creative Self-formation and positive social attitudes. What is always present in this case is the "I" and "Thou," the ego-Self axis, the personal and transpersonal, on which all development depends. The love learned in the primary relationship translates into the ability to accept the good and bad within oneself and the other. When this connection breaks, "the total personality sickens... instead of stressing the anthropocentric self-balance of the total personality, the accent shifts to the narcissistic ego centered on itself...to an asocial attitude and even to asocial behavior" (Neumann, 1966, p. 95).

A disturbance in the primary relationship may develop a neurosis that manifests as not being loved and a *primary sense of guilt*. This becomes a self-perception rather than a projection. A *secondary sense of guilt* arises with the introduction of the superego as the child moves closer to the patriarchy, building up moral aggressiveness towards him or herself. Narcissistic suffering results from the child's fearfulness and isolation, aggression and hostility, feeling bad and unwanted both consciously and unconsciously by the Terrible Mother. As a defensive compensation an ego-ideal is created as part of the persona. This leads the child to believe that he/she is independent, sufficient by themself, and perfect, an autocrat identified with the negative and sadistic side of the super-ego. By imposing a one-sided ideal on the ego that has nothing to do with the uniqueness of the individual, the natural processes of centroversion and automorphism are shut down and the child's narcissistic ego is instead ruled by the self-punishing shadow side of the super-ego. A reliance on the superego in opposition to the Self rather than the healthy ego, is also the status quo of patriarchal development resulting in a third form of guilt, *patriarchal guilt*:

> This "matricide," which corresponds to a turning away of masculine consciousness from the unconscious—the place of all peril, the seat of instincts, affects and transpersonal powers—leads in all patriarchal cultures to the "old" moral code typical for the West. Its goal is not that of automorphism, not the wholeness of a balanced personality directed by the ego-self axis and creatively related to other people, but rather a split personality

> determined by the ego-ideal and the superego. (Neumann, 1966, p. 99)

The shift from the old moral code as opposed to Neumann's new ethic as laid out in his book, *Depth Psychology and a New Ethic,* has been discussed in other chapters. It focuses not on the ethics of the superego but on an inner ethic that emerges from a heathy, discerning ego-Self axis.

Neumann drew a parallel between the injured negativistic ego and the patriarchal ego. Both can be considered neurotic in the sense that they split the opposites far apart. Not only do they have a profound effect on the individual's health, development and capacity for relationships, but also on cultural values and priorities. We witness these effects specifically regarding the exclusion and scapegoating of the feminine in our culture with its concomitant depreciation of the world, nature and the body. The isolation of the ego from the person is severe and includes a loss of relationship with the interior world. Those with a broken or nonexistent ego-Self axis feel lost, untethered, and are easily swayed by charismatic opinions or others' desires to destroy the existing order. Nothing is meaningful as in the postmodern view that anything is ok:[2]

> The narcissism of the negativistic ego is a typical expression of the lost conditions of modern man. His relationship to the "other," within and without, is lost and like the child disturbed in its primary relationship, he tries desperately, with the help of an inflated ego, to compensate for the lost ego-self relationship, and cannot see that the effort is hopeless. (Neumann, 1966, p. 102)

A one-sidedness on either side is dangerous—a splitting off of the Great Mother or Great Father. We need the parental whole to establish healthy individuals and cultures. The mass collectivization that we are witnessing now and what Neumann witnessed during WWII make clear that this individual self-loss leads to collective self-loss and disconnection of the unconscious. This then rises up from its shadow side with feelings of aggression, hatred and destruction. The feelings that underlie them all are fear, guilt, and anxiety, which are then projected out onto others. Is this how the evil that Neumann wrote about is generated or how its inherent existence is released into the world? The mechanism for its emanation is the loss of Self-formation and the defensive reaction to the split in individuals and the culture. This was evident in National Socialism and is evident today in our increasing autocratic world with calls for destruction:

> The restoration of the ego's relation to the self, the restoration of the ego-self axis, is identical with regaining that security of being which represents a unity of rational and irrational elements corresponding to the rational and irrational elements contained in the psychic totality of man. (Neumann, 1966, p.103)

We can psychologize about how to help the world heal, how to help humans move from one-sided patriarchy to a more integrated wholeness. It requires each person do the hard work of healing the splits and wounds that life has left us with by recognizing and assimilating our shadow side and complexes, and reestablishing the ego-Self axis through individuation to return to unitary reality in its conscious wholeness. This is very difficult work. Our world is moving in the opposite direction with scattered attention focused on our devices and social media. Our human brains are being programmed for a superficial horizontal consciousness devoid of the vertical depths—until the dragon of the neglected and repressed unconscious rears up and drags us down into anxiety, depression, and possible suicide. Many in the tech world long for *technological singularity,* when artificial intelligence surpasses human potential. This was not a worldly concern experienced by Neumann who died in 1960, but his clarity in describing what happens when the healthy stages of development are stifled point to the same individual and cultural catastrophes. We are witnessing this on a grand scale now.[3]

ENDNOTES

[1] Erel Shalit wrote a beautiful book on this topic, *A Story of Dreams, Fate and Destiny,* 2020 Zurich Lecture Series, Asheville, North Carolina: Chiron Publications.

[2] Nancy Furlotti, From Transiency to Healing in the Postmodern Condition. In Erel Shalit, 2018, *The Human Soul (Lost) in Transition at the Dawn of a New Era*. Asheville, North Carolina: Chiron Publications.

[3] For further insights and discussion on this topic, please refer to two chapters I wrote on narcissism. "Narcissism in the Home," and "Narcissism in Our Collective Home: Our American Culture", in *A Clear and Present Danger: Narcissism in the Era of Donald Trump,* 2016, pp. 149-171, pp. 201-212. (renamed, *A Clear and Present Danger: Narcissism in the Era of President Trump*, 2017 pp. 131-143, pp.191-202). Asheville, North Carolina: Chiron Publications.

CHAPTER VIII

Analysis of *The Great Mother*, and *Amor and Psyche: The Psychic Development of the Feminine*

Introduction

This chapter is an exploration into the world of the Great Mother, so important for our understanding of her relationship to both women and men. She sets the stage for all that develops out of nature and our instincts, as she is the primal earth and the matrix out of which everything grows and returns upon death. We will explore Erich Neumann's two books on the psychological development of the feminine, *The Great Mother* and *Amor and Psyche*: *The Psychic Development of the Feminine*. Each of us consists of psychological opposites, both feminine and masculine, and express each polarity in different ways. One thing is constant: both have their way with us. For the woman, her inner opposite is the animus. This represents her achievement of consciousness, developed beyond the hold of the Great Mother, or the unconscious. The unconscious is just that, unconscious, and wants things to stay that way. So, everything that emerges out of her is a struggle, a sacrifice, and runs the risk of regressing back to her.

Through the animus, a woman develops a connection to consciousness, which is the domain of the masculine—hard fought by him. This function, her inner opposite, helps her to think logically and act powerfully in the world with a will of her own, to express herself and ultimately find meaning. The animus acts as the bridge between the unconscious and conscious realms, as the guide or *psychopomp* to her development and eventual relationship to the greater Self. But before the animus steps into this role in her life, there is a lot of work to be done psychologically. The animus is always mixed with the shadow, inferior function and complexes, and this mess needs cleaned up and differentiated before the woman can establish herself with an ego strong enough to further her individuation journey.

The first part of the work is to help clarify, explore, express and sort out the seeds of confusion in her psyche from childhood and adult wounds. Differentiation is a function of consciousness: the introduction of a bit of light that gives her the ability to stand back and see things differently. This process is clearly described in alchemy, its stages of the work representing psychic development. As we know, most of our patients come to us in a state of *negredo* or depression or anxiety, in the dark unable to see any path forward—sad, overwhelmed and forlorn. We—and I say we because we have all been there—have been grabbed by the psyche when we lose our way and are thrown into the depth of despair, into the unconscious realm of the ruthless, terrible Great Mother. It is she who has us in her grip again. Only through suffering does the light of nature, the *lumen naturae* begin to sparkle in the psyche, on its own time, not ours. Then we can begin to glimpse a way forward. This light is the wisdom of the depths that speaks to us, in the form of the transformative Great Mother, perhaps in her animal form. It brings in a bit of the opposite, the light that leads us back to earth to help us establish a self (with the small "s"), spurred on our path of individuation by centroversion. This is the beginning, from *negredo* we move to *albedo*. With the introduction of light, we begin to see clearly. The development from then on is long and hard with lots of work to be done. We must avoid falling off or into many cliffs and caverns, back into the hell of darkness and the arms of the negative Great Mother, where no self-identity is possible.

The woman has to suffer and die many times in the process of change and transformation, unlike the man who goes on his hero's journey and kills off the dragon, boar, serpent or whale to escape the maternal hold. It is essential he do so to establish his own masculine identity separate from her. Since he is not of the same substance as his birth mother and the Great Mother, it is up to him to establish a relationship to the masculine, the patriarchy or Great Father, which reflects a move towards consciousness.

For the woman, it is not as essential because she is of the same nature as the Great Mother. A woman can live her entire life in the matriarchal womb, connected to the cycle of nature, the moon, giving birth, taking care of family and home. But she will never find her individual self. Many women don't have a need to do so. Of course, the undeveloped masculine/ animus within the woman may wreak havoc in her relationships because of it. In the same way, the man who remains the son-lover of the Great Mother, never taking on his heroic battle to escape her realm and join the conscious logos realm of the patriarchy, will not live his own life. He will pay for it through a negative anima, his own inner feminine. Just as the anima can spin webs of fear, inferiority, rejection and moodiness, the animus can be dictatorial, pointless, and circuitous in a fantasy-world of imagination, making no real sense other than as self-torture. The results are feelings of inferiority and incapacity, or projected judgmental anger out onto the other. In both cases, the shadow and complexes jump in to really do damage to relationships.

The feminine moves from identification with the Great Mother in the matriarchal uroboros—the mother/daughter dyad seen mythologically as Demeter/Kore—to experience the flash of inspiration and spiritual awakening in connection with the father in the patriarchal uroboros. This is the first glimpse of spiritual illumination, consciousness that grips her and shows her a further view of the world. Women do become fascinated with this stage and can remain there as the father's daughter, never progressing further. Either the father carries the projection of the animus or it moves to books or a spiritual quest—like nuns, who give up their lives for spirit as brides of Christ. This is considered to be the stage of the Oedipus complex, or desire for incest with the father. Of course, if stuck here in the patriarchal uroboros, the woman can remain in awe of men, maintain her projection onto the masculine and not learn to think for herself. If the animus flips into its negative side, she can become aggressive, ruthless, and brutal, having no real connection to conscious meaning but spouting rote, culturally correct diatribes that are judgmental and often offensive. At this point she is possessed by her animus. I'm sure we have all run across this type of woman or acted this way ourselves—

seductive around men or grandiose and a know-it-all. In this Patriarchal uroboros, the woman may be fascinated by the idealized masculine but at heart she is still caught in the matriarchal realm. While the negative Mother still maintains control of the masculine in the patriarchate as her son-lovers, women are also caught between the World Parents. Neumann pointed out the danger for a man who is caught in her web:

> A male immature in his development, who experiences himself only as male and phallic, perceives the feminine as a castrator, a murderer of the phallus. The projection of his own masculine desire and, on a still deeper level, of his own trend toward ouroboric incest, toward voluptuous self-dissolution in the primordial Feminine and Motherly, intensifies the terrible character of the Feminine. Thus, the Terrible Goddess rules over desire and over the seduction that leads to sin and destruction; love and death are aspects of one and the same Goddess. (Neumann, The Great Mother, 1981, p. 172)

It is vital for the man to also take that step towards differentiation, through his *dragon fight*, and to follow the lightning bolt of spirit towards consciousness. For the woman, there is continuing development beyond this first step into the patriarchate. As the woman moves away from identification with the good Mother and projection onto the good Father, centroversion pushes her further to find her own way, the path to uniting the opposites within, and this means not just the feminine and masculine but all the good and bad aspects, as well. Here she develops the ego-Self axis.

For men the process is led by the anima, the precious soul. Soul is psyche, meaning the totality. Pushing the man to develop, she manifests all the characteristics we speak of in relation to feminine psychology. She brings the man to his ability to experience a feeling-based reciprocal relationship, which balances out the lopsidedness of rational logos. For him, the process moves from the identification with the mother to finding his own footing separate from her, onto a loving relationship with the feminine both inside and in the real world. The real- world partner is very important in order to be mirrored by a *thou.*

The woman needs to develop her conscious logos side, her own ability to think and maintain her authority in the world, while the man needs to establish relationship to his heart and feeling. The woman moves toward meaning while the man moves toward image. The movement of centroversion, which establishes a balance between introversion and extroversion, leads her toward consciousness while the man moves away from it, toward relationship to nature and his soul.

The last stage of development for the woman is a transformation in spirit/logos. It is the ego-Self relationship, where the greater Self is the dynamic force, containing the totality of spirit and the wisdom of Sophia. This is a union of rational and heart consciousness, the light from above connected with the light from below—the *lumen naturae.* This union of spirit and nature is represented in the tree of life that has roots in heaven and in the earth.

An Overview of the Archetype of The Great Mother

The uroboros, the snake biting its tail, also called the Great Round, is the universe and container for everything at the early primal stage of existence. It is the chaos at the beginning of creation when nothing is yet differentiated. Archetypal Feminine and Masculine are present in a great mixing bowl. The Archetypal Feminine is the overarching energy containing the aspects of the Great Mother who emerges as heaven, water, earth and even fire as her son. Out of the Great Mother, goddess of time and the moon, everything is born and returns to her in death. The feminine energy present from the beginning consists of the good, the terrible and the *good-bad* Mother. Three goddesses are represented here: Isis, the Gorgon, and Sophia. The Gorgon is the terrible mother, Sophia is the good mother while Isis is both, corresponding to the Great Mother. These aspects are in command before the dragon fight with the male hero.

The Feminine is both elementary and transformative. By elementary we mean the container or vessel holding everything connected to the earth, the original foundation ground of the feminine. It is the egg, the woman=body=vessel=world, creative principle. The transformative nature of the feminine is the dynamic element of the psyche that drives change and transformation. This is seen in giving birth but also as the instigator of change that encourages the male—and male aspect in the female—to undertake the search for soul and spirit. It is the mover of all action and creation in the inner and outer world. It is higher than the elemental mother whose symbols are the womb and belly, while the transformative mother is symbolized by the breasts, heart and mouth. It is important to note that the anima is concerned with the individual man and his development, while the Great Mother is not concerned with the independence of the individual or the ego. She would just as soon keep him with her. It is the anima that confronts the man with a *trial,* as it also is with the animus. Both the good and terrible mother can be either elemental or transformational. And sometimes it is the negative Mother who is the one who is the most transformational.

Neumann clarified the relationship between the Archetypal Feminine and Archetypal Masculine:

> At one pole stands the goddess as elementary, material, and natural reality. As we approach the other pole, there is a progressive abstraction from the material; the spirit tends to become "pure" spirit, pure dynamic without material substratum. But this second pole is no longer within the scope of the Archetypal Feminine; it belongs to the specific form of the Masculine, as most fully manifested in the world of the patriarchal spirit. (1981, n. 34, p. 108)

The spiritual symbol of the matriarchal is the moon and the night sky, while for the patriarchal it is lightening and the sun. Birth and rebirth are always related to the matriarchal transformation. "The breath-logos sequence, like many other symbols and symbol groups, was later appropriated by the patriarchate, but it everywhere reveals its matriarchal origin" (1981, p. 61). Inspiration comes from the spiritual aspect of the feminine, Sophia, and is felt through the anima. Yet the relation between the Feminine and the spiritual-Masculine begins with the paternal uroboros, which is the transpersonal principle seen as *spirit-wind* and is the first step towards differentiation driven by centroversion. Later the masculine transforms in the patriarchate as *spirit-sun* (1981, n. 22, p. 294). How did the patriarchy emerge out of the matriarchy? Neumann explained:

> The male proceeds to deny the genetic principle which is precisely the basic principle of the matriarchal world. Or, mythologically speaking, he murders his mother and undertakes the patriarchal revaluation by which the son identified with the father makes himself the source from which the Feminine—like Eve arising from Adam's rib—originated in a spiritual and antinatural way. (1981, p. 58)

And later the significance of the vessel is reversed as birth giver, to become a container that serves to house and feed instead. It is clear that the struggle between the feminine and masculine has been going on from the beginning!

The Feminine Mysteries

The feminine spiritual mysteries consist of the vegetative mysteries having to do with fertility, growth and increase of life; the Eleusinian mysteries having to do with Demeter and Persephone are representative. The Terrible Mother is in charge of the Death mysteries having to do with the fertilization of the earth, care of the dead, and sacrifices leading to death. This is based on the cycle of seasonal growth in nature—from the planting of seeds to sprouting to growth, and finally death of the plant when it is cut down. Then we have the inspirational mysteries of Dionysus, bound up with male-spiritual power and the paternal uroboros and the ecstatic, orgiastic nature of the Feminine. The feminine spirit culminates in vision, inspiration, and the birth of the divine child—the son reflecting the unconscious spiritual aspect of herself or the daughter, representing her feminine Self. The other side of this has to do with intoxication mysteries. The Pythia at Delphi, for example, used substances to induce visions and tell the future. Delphi originally had a temple dedicated to Dionysus, and later one dedicated to Apollo. Intoxication mysteries are quite the rage in the US with all the research now being done on the use of psilocybin, LSD and MDMA to treat depression, PTSD, and end of life issues. When seized during one of these mysteries, or on one of these drugs, it can be by the positive or negative side of the feminine archetype—encounters with the witch or Sophia—that one experiences. The purpose is to stimulate transformation through a sudden and forceful breaking down of the present personality structure. This would allow the light of consciousness to burst through and open a wider view of the world through the influx of spirit—both feminine and masculine. This influx can also be their dark, negative sides resulting in madness. The ultimate purpose of these mysteries is initiation or rebirth into a wider, expanded consciousness. As discussed previously, one needs to be careful with psychedelics.

The symbols change through this long process of psychological development of the feminine: from cosmic egg at the beginning to the sacred white rose, flower of light, and white dove, messenger of the Holy Ghost and Sophia, offering the wisdom of the heart and feeling, not the rational wisdom of logos and the head.

What is important to remember is that we live in a world ruled by the values of the Patriarchy, while underneath lies the raging anger of the dispossessed Matriarchy. The goddesses were rejected, killed in the dragon fights, pushed back into the unconscious to seethe and plot. Their faces were those of Medea, Medusa, Kali, and all the witches. Slowly as the Patriarchy has moved to its extreme of rational logos thinking and empirical science—resulting in wars, nuclear bombs, the denigration and destruction of our natural world, and the removal of women's rights—the Great Mother is creeping out of the shadows where she has spun her angry, evil mischief for so long. She is activating the feminine in women and men to not deny their feeling hearts and pay attention to the importance of their natural surroundings. We are now in the midst of global climate change, the Covid-19 pandemic, and the war in Ukraine. These challenges are bringing to light what has been missing in our cultural one-sided view. This opens a path to potentially bring the

Feminine and Masculine archetypes together on a collective level. It is no easy feat. Just as the negative Great Mother fights to keep her own, so the negative Great Father does the same by trying to suppress his opposite: her. It must be remembered that one aspect of the negative Masculine remains a part of the Feminine, ruled from the unconscious as her destructive male companion. These are her warriors, her Berserkers—as men or as animus. They are the fierce undeveloped masculine that remain under her control. This is still present psychologically and accounts for a lot of destruction and killing.

The goal of centroversion is active in the psyche from the beginning, leading to the establishment of the ego-Self relationship. Individuation takes place in the second half of life, pushing us to strive to bring the opposites of matter and spirit, the conscious and unconscious realms, together after their long separation, creating a new third element out of the original two. This is the transcendent function. Only then will the Great Father and Great Mother be recognized as part of a whole as the Great Parents, far removed from the chaos in the beginning, now in differentiated form expressing the wisdom of logos and the heart.

On Neumann's Diagrams

In his book, *The Great Mother*, Neumann presents three diagrams which explain the archetypal world, including the Feminine and the Masculine:
Schema I (p. 18): He lays out a map of the World at the top with the projected figures like: Human Being, Sophia, Gorgon and Isis Consciousness. Under that is Consciousness and the Unconscious, including Anima. Next down is The Great Mother including, Terrible Mother, Great Mother and Good Mother. Beneath that is the Archetypal Feminine. Then below that is The Uroboros and at the bottom is The Archetype and The Unconscious.
Schema II (p. 44): He draws a depiction of the symbolical Alchemical Universe beginning at the top with: Heaven, including the Moon and its three phases. Under that is the World: with cities, houses, vegetation, nature, well and symbolism related to: the Sun, soma, medicine, host, crown. The third section under the world consists of the Alchemical Work

in the vessel and symbolism having to do with: the earth, water, pond, ocean, animals, the body, vessel, egg cave, mountain, etc. The bottom layer consists of the Underworld: hell, grave, urn, night, darkness, the chasm and maw. Neumann shows how they ae all interconnected from the bottom up to the Retort, Grail, Logos, Wisdom and Water of life

Schema III (p. 83): Neumann draws the many facets of the Archetypal Feminine, both positive and negative, in a large circle containing all aspects of goddesses, mysteries, transformation processes: At the top is the *Positive Feminine* F+, represented by the mother, virgin, Mary and Demeter on one side, and Mary and Sophia on the other. On the *Positive Mother side M+, Good Mother* is listed with the Vegetation mysteries with Demeter, Isis, (Ishtar, Kwan-yin, Shekinah) immortality, rebirth, birth, fruit, development, bearing/releasing. The *Positive Archetypal side A+, transformative character*, is listed with the Inspiration mysteries and Mary, Sophia, Muses, (Athena, Artemis, Kore) wisdom, vision, inspiration, ecstasy, transformation, sublimation, giving.

On the *Negative Mother side M-, the Terrible Mother*, is listed: Kali, Gorgon, Hecate, (Ishtar, Isis, Artemis, Erinyes, Furies, Lamias, witches) the Death mysteries, dismemberment, death, extinction, sickness, diminution, fixating, ensnaring.

On the *Negative Archetypal side A-, the Negative Transformative character* are: Lilith, Circe, Astarte, (Aphrodite, Artemis, the Lorelei, Medea, elves, sprites) Mysteries of drunkenness, ecstasy, madness, impotence, stupor, transformation, dissolution, rejection, deprivation. At the bottom is located the *Negative Feminine N-* as: the young and old witch. The center circle is the Elementary Character represented by containing. The circle widens to the next inner layer, Transformation, then outside of that is Spiritual Transformation moving upward into consciousness.

These three schemas are complicated to describe yet well thought out and clearly presented, worthwhile to examine.

On The Myth of Amor and Psyche

Now we will turn to the myth of *Amor and Psyche: The Psychic Development of the Feminine* that Neumann published in German in 1952 and in English in 1956. This myth gives us a visual, felt experience of the stages of conscious development, much like the very early myth of Osiris, and Neumann's look at the development of the masculine. Nevertheless, both these myths reflect the development of the feminine and the masculine.

The myth begins with Aphrodite jealous of this creature called Psyche, the human with exceptional beauty. This causes mortal men to neglect her cult and instead travel on pilgrimages to see Psyche. This is an affront to the Aphrodite, the Goddess of Beauty. To punish Psyche for her beauty and transgression, Aphrodite asks her son, Eros, to avenge her by making Psyche fall in love with a vile man. On the earthly realm, Psyche is surprisingly not the object of any man's love. Her own father, wondering why, takes her to an oracle to find the answer. It is revealed that she will be abandoned to the marriage of death with a monster. What a horrible yet mysterious fate.

Eros, following his mother's wishes, captures Psyche and flies her on his wings to his lofty home high on top of the mountain, keeping her for himself as his plaything. He visits her only at night and will not allow her to see his face ever. If she tries, he warns her, he will leave and never return. They live in sexual bliss with Eros' nightly visits until Psyche's stepsisters, wondering where she is, track her down. They taunt her into believing Eros is really that prophetic monster, a snake or dragon. They are jealous of her rich and sumptuous life in this palatial home high on the mountain that she shares with him. These sisters, as envious as they are, also represent a shadow aspect of Psyche that wants out of her sensual prison. They encourage Psyche to look at him in secret, and if he is a monster, to kill him.

One night she takes a knife in one hand and a lantern in the other, which she holds close to his face while he is sleeping. She sees that he is beautiful and not a monster at all. In pulling the knife closer to herself, away from him, she slips. She spills a drop of hot lantern oil onto Eros's shoulder, burning him terribly. He immediately wakes up, sees her looking at him and flees. She, of course, is now totally despondent at losing her beloved.

Immediately realizing what happened, Aphrodite swooshes in and taunts the poor young girl, tearing her clothes, throwing her about and disheveling her hair. Aphrodite orders a punishment in the form of a task: she has to sort a mixed-up mound of corn, barley, millet, poppy seeds, chick peas, lentils and beans. Aphrodite screeches that this job suits an ugly serving-wench like Psyche, and she must finish it by the evening. Of course, the poor girl is distraught and overwhelmed, not knowing what to do—so lost and feeling forlorn. Miraculously, little ants come to her aid and do the sorting for her, completing the job on time. After seeing this, Aphrodite is furious.

Eros, meanwhile, is kept in his room away from any possible encounter with Psyche that could reignite their passions toward each other. He is weak and suffering from the burn on his shoulder. Aphrodite then gives Psyche a second task: obtain a piece of the special golden wool from the sheep that live on the banks of a stream sourced by high mountain water. Again forlorn, Psyche has no idea how she could succeed with this task and thinks of throwing herself off the mountain to her death, when a green reed begins to speak to her, giving her instructions on obtaining a tuft of wool from the aggressive and dangerous sheep. She is instructed to approach them in the afternoon when they have retreated to avoid the hot sun, and the cool breezes have lulled them to sleep. While safe from their madness and anger, she can creep over to the branch of a tree nearby and find a tuft of wool hanging to take to the Great Goddess.

Once again Aphrodite is furious although a bit bemused at the girl's success. She gives Psyche a third task: she now has to go to the top of the mountain, to the source of the stream, and bring back a jar or urn of water. Psyche sees how difficult this task is going to be and the thought of death again is ever present. She is beyond having tears to cry—so overwhelmed with peril. Then from the sky, the royal bird of Zeus comes to her aid. The eagle helps her get the Stygian waters from the River Styx—the waters of the Gods and the underworld. The bird takes the urn, fills it with the water and gives it to Psyche.

With this success, she is still not able to appease the vengeful Goddess, Aphrodite, who then gives her a final task. Now Psyche has to take a casket and descend into the underworld. She is to present it to Persephone so that she can fill it with enough of her beauty to last

Aphrodite one day. This Goddess of Beauty is worn out looking after her saddened and sick son. Psyche is now sure her luck has come to its end and that she is doomed. It is an impossible task to go into the underworld, into Tartarus. Once again, she is about to throw herself off a tower when that very edifice begins to speak to her, to admonish her to not harm herself but to follow its advice. It gives her the directions she needs to enter one of the gaping portals to the underworld, the vent of Dis. She will have to continue on, but not empty-handed.

She needs to take cakes kneaded of pearl barley and mead, and carry in her mouth two coins. She is counseled that on her way she will come across a lame ass bearing wood on its back with a lame driver. He will ask her to hand him a few twigs that have fallen from the load. She should ignore him and not speak. Then she will come to the river of the dead where Charon will ask the ferryman's toll before he will take a traveler to the far shore. She must pay him one of the coins from her mouth. As she travels in the boat, a dead man floating in the river will ask for a hand, but she is not to help him. Next, the three old women as they weave their web, will ask for her help but she must not touch their web. Finally, there will appear a huge hound with three heads, wild and terrible, that bays with a thunderous roar. He guards the empty house of Dis. She is to give him a cake to eat and she will be able to pass by him with ease and enter into Persephone's house.

Persephone will appear with a kindly manner inviting Psyche to sit and eat a feast with her, but the tower tells her to sit on the floor instead and ask for course-bread to eat. Now is the time for Psyche to ask for what she wants and then depart, returning the way she came and paying off the foes she encountered along the way. She manages to leave safely but then is tempted by her own thoughts, her own curiosity about what she is carrying in her arms—Persephone's divine beauty ointment. What girl could resist this? Vanity and curiosity win, and she unclasps the casket and finds nothing inside but the death sleep of the underworld. She immediately falls down and sleep possesses her completely— now she is nothing more than a sleeping corpse.

It just so happens that Eros has finally recovered from his burn from the drop of oil Psyche had spilled on him. He is now refreshed and energized, and slips out of his bedroom window, flying as fast as he can to Psyche's side. He wipes the Stygian sleep off her and puts it back in the casket, and then she awakes to the prick of one of his arrows. He tells her to hurry to complete this fourth task and that he will meet her there. Before going, he flies to Mount Olympus and beseeches Zeus to protect Psyche from his mother. Eros is Zeus's son, and he is happy to comply as long as the next beautiful girl Eros runs across will be given to him. Zeus gathers all the Gods on high, and they take a vote to confirm that Psyche will remain with Eros and become immortal. Aphrodite's concerns and anger are now assuaged. Having been pregnant all along, Psyche and Eros have a daughter whom they name Pleasure or Joy.

On The Interpretation/Amplification of the Myth

This myth lays out the steps taken in a feminine or matriarchal initiation. Aphrodite is an aspect of the Great Mother. She is both good—full of love and sensuality and attraction—and terrible and vengeful. It is this second aspect that Psyche has to encounter and somehow overcome. Psyche's fault was beauty. The Great Mother and her son-lover Amor/Eros had to punish her for this human hubris. I prefer to call him Eros. At this early point in the myth, he is a head-strong, *wicked boy* whose arrows threaten both his mother Aphrodite and his father Zeus. He too needs an initiation into maturity and needs to separate from his mother/lover.

Every feminine initiation begins with death—the marriage with death. For example, this is seen in the myth of the Kore or Persephone when she is kidnapped and taken into the underworld by Hades/Dionysus and raped. This is replayed in the Eleusinian Kore/Demeter mysteries where Persephone is stolen from her mother Demeter. It is felt as something stolen because the elemental Great Mother doesn't give up what is hers easily. This motif of the marriage of death is at the heart of the feminine initiation. The primordial identity between the mother and daughter is fundamental and needs to be broken in order for the daughter to find her own identity and follow her own path of individuation. In this myth

Persephone lives half the year in the underworld with Hades as his wife and Goddess of the underworld, and half the year on the earth with her mother Demeter, the Goddess of nature, the Great Mother. She has brought together an important set of opposites—establishing an ego-Self axis.

This pattern of change and growth is so true for feminine development. Women are identified with their mothers because they are both of the same gender. There is no sense of *other* in that relationship. Because of this It is easy to remain in the matriarchal uroboros as part of the elemental feminine and follow the mother's path, the same path that many generations of women followed—marrying, having babies, caring for their husbands and dying. This myth brings in a new psychological attitude to shift the development of the individual away from being merely a part of the cycle of nature, to move her out of identification with the Great Mother to find her own unique self.

Psyche struggles with death throughout the myth. She starts out in participation mystique with the Great Mother—merely being and doing what she was told to do. She feels, though, as if she were dead inside, being unwanted and unloved by any man until she's carried off by Eros. While interesting and seductive, he still is not real enough for her, not related in an intimate, genuine way. She could not even see his face. Something within her, an inner curiosity, an inner strength pushes her to challenge the status quo—to not be the obedient girl but to push back. Granted, in the myth it was her sisters who pushed her to look at the monster, but they represent shadow aspects in her that question and want answers. The sisters were envious and hateful, but those qualities, too, are important bits of shadow that will get us into trouble. It is trouble we need to make to develop the ego-Self axis. As girls, without our attitudes, pushiness, curiosity, creativity and inner knowing that there is more to life than conforming and doing what our mothers and grandmothers did, we would remain in the maternal uroboros living in the elemental world.

As a personal example, I was raised a Mormon and was told all my life that my goal in life should be to get married and have lots of children—that was it! My mother and grandmother plotted in the hopes of securing this future for me. I, however, was more of a *tomboy* and had very little interest in girlie things. I was athletic and strong, always outside riding my bike or horses or playing sports, not playing house with dolls. I was more of an Artemis child/woman of nature. Home was not such a safe place, actually. Something inside me was *me* from my beginning and no matter how the women in my life did not like it, there was nothing they could do to change that internal compass determined to push me to find out who I was and to eventually grow into my genuine self. This was the guiding force of centroversion in my psyche. I certainly did not want to be them. My mother kept asking me for years when I was going to give up my silliness of working and being a psychologist. Wasn't I happy in the home, wasn't that enough? I managed to separate from her but she never managed to separate from me. I remained a projection of herself. Even on her deathbed when she was asked by her caretaker who I was— pointing at me sitting across the room from her—she looked over at me and said, "Why, that's me!" She lived in the patriarchate with an eye toward the obedience and conformity to the father's rules, with one foot in the matriarchal uroboros of the good and terrible mother. She never managed to separate from the Great Parents to find her own standpoint. She never even knew one might want to escape. We all have our stories of captivity and rebellion. The many people we work with in therapy continue to come because something inside whispers that there may be a different way. The inner process of centroversion strives to establish a connection between the psyche and the outer world of rules, guidelines for living and the conscious collective. After this difficult work of differentiation, individuation moves us toward a reconciliation of opposites through the transcendent function to form a conscious wholeness—as opposed to the unity of chaos with which we were born. Both are represented by the uroboros.

Psyche's fate was to escape both the matriarchal and the patriarchal and offer humanity a new path. She rebelled against both. Her encounter with Eros seemed like paradise, all too perfect until her sisters, like the snake in the Garden of Eden, emerged to challenge this *perfection*. Her so–called marriage to Eros was really slavery to the Great Mother. She was his slave, and he remained a slave to his mother. It is always a snake that appears from the unconscious to bring new messages—to terrify and challenge us to shed our old skins and struggle to discover the new way and new attitude. This snake energy breaks in unannounced and unwanted but so necessary. Deep from our instinctual, primordial earthly nature, from the positive, transformative aspect of Great Mother herself, it emerges to lead us to ourselves. While Aphrodite seems to behave like the negative Great Mother in all her rage and hatred and belittling, she still carries the transformative element—this is the negative transformative element. But it certainly gets one's attention when we encounter this energy. It takes a blast of destruction to put us on a different path. There is definitely a place for the soft Good Mother and she is very important, but for transformation we need that angry part.

Any increase in consciousness is a loss for the Great Mother. She fundamentally tries to keep what is hers in the unconscious. Knowing this, the emergence of the patriarchy had to be brutal in pushing her away, demonizing her and all the incredible Great Mother Goddesses of the Middle East like Ishtar, Astarte, Isis-Sophia and Aphrodite. They were all-powerful early on and had to be subdued in order for consciousness to ascend to create the patriarchal cultures represented by the monotheistic religions. It was a raging struggle for centuries. Finally the female goddesses pushed into the underworld reappeared as Medea, Medusa and Sekmet—the negative opposite of Isis. The ignored female goddesses became angry, ruthlessly lurking in the shadows ready to cause trouble. They were split off and as a result, Eros, love, relationship and pleasure was imprisoned by the monotheistic beliefs of the patriarchy.

Exploring this myth and similarities regarding the feminine mysteries is just as relevant for the masculine and male initiation—it can be read from both perspectives. While Psyche is the whole of the unconscious, the anima is a significant piece of the feminine that brings all these feminine qualities and sensibilities to the man to guide him to wholeness. Just as Psyche had to metaphorically die in her struggle to discover her strengths, including a connection to nature through the ants and eagle, she also had to learn about logos through the tower that guided her. She had to work on both her feminine and masculine parts to ultimately find her own wholeness, which is her divinity bestowed upon her at the conclusion of this tale.

The man follows a more spiritual heroic path, while hers is of the earth. He has to find spirit and soul to come to his wholeness. It is through his anima's struggle to make a place for herself in his psyche that he finds love, Eros, and Pleasure. It is through her that he finds his soul.

We see this path clearly in *The Red Book* when Jung is faced with Salome, brought along by Elijah. Jung is furious and asks why he has brought this despicable woman with him as a companion. How could this be? She was the one responsible for the death of John the Baptist; she had his head cut off. He wants nothing to do with her. She is blind at this point, meaning unconscious. Jung sees her as all seduction and earthly pleasure. What also came along with Salome and Elijah was a snake. Always, presence of the snake is transformation to be had. Jung spends a lot of time talking to this snake, this chthonic creature with the wisdom of the earth, the Great Mother and nature. That is not the realm of the masculine but it is what the man needs to feel and experience. It is the anima that guides the man through his psychological process to pleasure, to joy, to love, to relationship. Finally, through many abominations and tortures, Jung is hung on a cross like Christ and Mithras. From his suffering and forced acceptance of his soul, Salome gains her sight. In other words, his anima becomes conscious.

Pure physical pleasure and lust transform into his ability to experience joy and love for the other. For the man, the anima is experienced through real relational encounters and because of his work on the inner anima he is able to open to love and compassion when relationship is presented. For Jung, his soul appeared as the snake and as the bird, depending on whether he needed knowledge from the chthonic realm or from the spirit realm. It is a bridging of the two that balances the personality and results in the *hieros gamos*, the wholeness of spirit and nature—Psyche and Eros.

We can look at this myth of Psyche and Eros in relation to feminine and masculine development. Basically, we all need both to become whole. We just get there in different ways. Eros in this myth can be the animus of the woman or the ego/self of the man. Early in the myth he is really a little boy, just wanting to play around and not take life too seriously. He annoys his parents by shooting his arrows indiscriminately, creating a bit of chaos with his power. He, too, needs to grow up. It is his anima, his soul that does all the work, and for him it is an inner transformation that takes place while he lies wounded from the hot oil and captive of his mother/lover. He is the son who needs to escape and when he is strong enough, he flies out the window to gain his independence from the Great Mother. He heads directly to his partner and lover Psyche and brings her back to life, which only he is capable of doing. The man awakens the woman and the woman awakens the man. They are each other's inner opposites. They have transcended both the matriarchy and patriarchy and found relationship to each other—the bridge that includes both. The union of the two is Pleasure, or joy. This child of that name emerges from her mother, who struggled with death and depression, and her father, who was too flighty and lofty to be grounded enough for real joy and relationship. Pleasure represents the new third transcendent function, bridging the opposites between her parents.

The sisters represent the matriarchate, hating the men, wanting to kill or castrate them. Their own husbands are boring slave drivers that they must care for without love or passion. They are victims locked in the elemental world of the feminine. Here we have all the symbolism of blind obedience, castration, domination, captivity and helplessness. We see these images frequently in dreams where the woman is held captive or pursued by a dangerous man who wants to hurt her. For men, this is the fear of the feminine through fear of being castrated, controlled, or told he is a weak little boy. He fears being dragged back into the world of the mother as captive son/lover. This fundamental fear of the feminine plays out in men who do not own their true power or self-determination. Their animas are deeply buried in the unconscious, never having separated from the Great Mother or Great Father. They pass laws demanding that women cover themselves up, not to be seen because they are too seductive; they suppress the feminine because it is dangerous. Removing women's control over their own bodies, they seek to keep them in the home, *barefoot and pregnant* with freedom lost. It is the fight between the patriarchy and matriarchy that still plays out where men and women have not done their psychological work, which is most of the world.

This is getting worse in my country now with the rise of the Alt-right male, the Evangelical White Nationalist Christian men who want to keep the feminine suppressed at all costs. This is seen as they take away medical care for women, and all possible female rights. When men feel insecure, it is women who pay the price. The opposite is true, too, as they themselves suffer their tyrannical animas who hate men! All negatives get projected onto the woman just as historically they have onto all the powerful and threatening Great Goddesses. Women have too much control, they think. It is true that women create life, and as nature herself, have the ability to take it away. The feminine does control the cycle of life, like the seed of corn that is planted and then cut down at the end of summer. The matriarchy runs on the moon cycle and the seasons. The patriarchy, as sun and spirit, strives to control nature, to civilize and create order with laws and rules in order to be superior to all beneath it—which means standing on the carcasses of the old maternal order.

Psyche emerges from her matriarchal bed fired up as a man-hater with knife and lantern light ready to kill the dragon Eros. When she snaps out of her captivity and sees for the first time her very own Eros the God, she is seized from within with love, not only from without as passion. She loves for the first time, no longer just captive or captivating. Now she must suffer her real feeling as Neumann pointed out in Amor and Psyche:

> Love as an expression of wholeness is not possible in the dark, as a merely unconscious process; an authentic encounter with another involves consciousness, hence also the aspect of suffering and separation....Now begins the age of human love, when the human psyche consciously takes the fateful decision on itself. Psyche becomes the new Aphrodite as opposed to Aphrodite as the Great Mother. (1973, pp. 85-86)

Aphrodite, the Great Mother, was born of the union of sky and sea, while Psyche is a product of a union between heaven and earth. The development in this myth ends with the deification of the human Psyche. She is the one who has humanized the gods. Neumann has made this point before in his earlier works, showing how humans play an important role in bringing consciousness to God.

On her journey, she passes through the four elements, creating a mandala of wholeness in her travails. First, she encounters the ants that order the seeds of the earth. Then she encounters the talking reeds of the vegetative world and domain of water to help her retrieve a piece of the golden wool. This is infused with the destructively bright sun consciousness of the Ram, a symbol for Aries, the fiery lover of Aphrodite. She moves further into the animal spirit layer with the eagle of Zeus, into the world of instinct and air, the unconscious masculine spirit. The eagle carrying her urn signifies that her development is manifesting a first union of opposites represented by the feminine container, her vessel of individuation, and the masculine spirit, the eagle, filling it with the water of life.

Finally, it is the tower that directs her on her dangerous and complicated journey into the underworld. The tower represents both masculine and feminine. As mandala container and phallic earth spirit, it is the far-seeing tower. In her last task she has to face the feminine directly as the archetype of Persephone-Aphrodite herself. Here, no animal can help her. She has to go herself to retrieve something hidden from the underworld and bring it intact up to earth. Along the way she cannot allow herself to be distracted by relatedness. She has to be tough and keep her eyes on her long goal, not what is close at hand. This is a very difficult snag that our patients run into frequently. They get distracted by the Great Mother who wants to keep us unconscious. For example, perhaps one should leave a marriage or unhealthy relationship but pity keeps us there. The feminine, as woman or anima, needs to develop a toughness to be able to make the right decision, able to differentiate between opposites—an aspect of the development of her masculine side and consciousness. She no longer blindly follows the demands of her matriarchal instincts alone, or the rules of the patriarchy and super-ego. She makes her own decisions as a sign of ego stability and resilience. Psyche is accompanied by unconsciousness, the Self, throughout her journey while her ego follows. Her ego is certainly not directing the action as it would in a man's heroic journey, like that of Odysseus, Heracles or Perseus. She is challenged with masculine tasks as a way of developing that side of herself, and yet remains true to her feminine side. She now has conscious access to both, establishing the ego-Self axis.

At this stage the Eros relatedness component is accompanied by masculine spirit, which at first is unconscious but becomes increasingly more conscious as Psyche is challenged. Eros, when he flew away to hide is passive but transformed through Psyche's efforts, or the efforts of his anima as a projection of Psyche. She confronts love and hate, light and dark, consciousness and unconsciousness as the opposites come into conflict with each other time after time. She is bringing the opposites together and separating from the original parents, the Great Mother and the Great Father, becoming her own person through both love for Eros and love for herself.

The final task is interesting. You'd think at this point she would have learned to follow instructions carefully but the death pull, a regression to the unconscious, is too great. She has been drawn to it all along, struggling to stand on her own. She fails and falls into a regression, a deathly sleep, not fully able to leave the underworld. Like Persephone herself who ate a pomegranate and was doomed to remain there for half the year, Eurydice had to remain in the underworld when her husband Orpheus looked back to see her on their journey out. Aphrodite finally caught her on her last task, to keep her captive in her role of Great Mother of death. But for a woman on her psychological path, it is failure and acceptance that results in success. Women must learn to accept the dragon, not to slay it.

Psyche began her journey with the light of the lantern wanting to see Eros, and she ends with what could be seen as failure in the total blackness of this deathlike sleep. But from here she is able to reconnect with Eros, as her own inner spirit as animus—who also now appreciates this new middle ground between heaven and the underworld. In this newfound place between opposites, Psyche exhibits love that only exists in the human realm. This is the feminine mystery of rebirth through love.

And what part does Aphrodite play in this story? She clearly is the archaic Terrible Mother to Psyche, but she is also very much the Transformative Mother because she sets Psyche on her path of individuation. And to Eros she is the Good Mother through her care, but it is too much really, and therefore she is more like the mother/lover holding her son captive. In this role she is the too positive mother who turns into the negative elemental Mother by stifling his development in hope of keeping him for herself.

The Great Mother may appear as a figure of the feminine side of the Self or as the archetype itself. This archetype contains the opposition of Aphrodite-Fortuna or bad fortune, as well as Isis-Sophia or good fortune. The opposition of the positive and negative sides of the Great Mother archetype are clearer in masculine psychology. In the patriarchy, there is a simpler opposition, with the negative Mother rejected and thrust back into the unconscious. For the woman it is more difficult because she must unite all aspects of this archetype within herself—all the various Goddesses of ancient Greece, for example. Together they make up the wholeness of the archetype of the Great Mother for the woman.

The psychological development of the woman moves from mother-daughter in the uroboros to self-ego in the matriarchy but with the Great Mother still the dominant figure. The next phase is the paternal uroboros to arrive at the psychology of the patriarchy and the dominance of the Great Father. We live in a world dominated by this stage: the thoughts and values of the rational mind determine our culture through our super-ego and empirical world view. The woman also needs to overcome the patriarchal domination that results in being aligned with spirit and reason at the expense of feminine feeling and instincts. The Great Parents must be overcome to establish the individual. Increasingly today we are seeing the emergence of that important stage of development that we saw in the myth of Psyche and Eros. This is the encounter between the two values, masculine and feminine. The feminine is finding her feminine Self in the light of day, out of the darkness and in relationship with the opposite.

In our myth this is seen in the behavior of the hostile sisters. Moving from the Matriarchy to Patriarchy was a necessary and important development individually and culturally to establish civilization, but now we need to take that next step to integrate both. We see this age old struggle between opposites still present and acting out alongside movement toward integration of the two archetypal energies. As positive as it is that women are finding their sense of wholeness, the backlash against this is increasingly apparent in the masculine desire to silence women. The regression seems to express a fear of change and the destructive angry power of the feminine, with a desire to hold to the older set of Patriarchal rules. The feminine also tried to hold what was hers when it was being taken away.

Just as it is difficult to fully "distinguish[ing] between the progressive character of the Self and the regressive nature of the Great Mother archetype" (Neumann, 1973, pp. 131-132), it is difficult to distinguish what is animus as opposed to the larger influences of the masculine archetypes and spirit. This is the patriarchal uroboros that works at the edges of the animus. Psyche had to touch on all these energies and incorporate her own masculine principles before she was able to confront the opposing sides of the Great Mother, positive and negative. This allowed her to come into contact with her true Self and her loving soul. Her journey is through death to rebirth and resurrection. Suffering, transformation and illumination leads to her becoming divine and giving birth to a child, who is *the treasure hard to attain*. This is the mystery of her initiation and the template for feminine development.

Conclusion

The importance of human love was celebrated in the art, culture and mysticism of the middle-ages with the troubadours, Dante's love for Beatrice, and Faust's Eternal Feminine (Neumann, 1973, p.139). You have all the stories of the Knights in Shining Armor protecting the fair women with their lives. These works projected all the positive and vulnerable qualities of these women for the first time in history. They became precious jewels to be guarded and cared for, not touched but looked at. At this time the story of Perceval and the Quest for the Holy Grail was written[1], laying out the psychological process of masculine development circling around the feminine vessel. Psyche and Eros was far earlier and a precursor of what was to come for feminine development. The birth of the baby girl named Pleasure or Joy is an interesting twist in the story. Rather than the birth of the animus-spirit, the girl represents a far more integral part of Psyche's feminine self and wholeness.

The mythical birth of the godhead for a man does not take place in the anima but in the psyche as the birth of the totality. Neumann explained:

> The feminine mysteries, like what we have seen here and in the Eleusinian Isis/Demeter mysteries, differ essentially from the masculine-patriarchal mysteries. The masculine mystery is bound up with the active heroic struggle of the ego and is based on the central insight that "I and the father are one". But the primordial feminine mysteries have a different structure. They are mysteries of birth and rebirth and appear predominantly in three different forms: as birth of the logos, son of light; as birth of the daughter, the new Self; and as birth of the dead in rebirth. Where ever we find this elementary feminine symbolism, we have—psychologically speaking—matriarchal mysteries, regardless of whether those initiated are men or women. (1973, p. 148-149)

It is important to note that the psyche for men and women is feminine. This seems obvious but because of the structural differences that emerge psychologically between the feminine and masculine it may not be clear. The background matrix for both is the psyche or the unconscious. This psyche represents soul which is the amniotic fluid that we all symbolically reside in and are born out of physically and psychologically. Through the stages of psychological development women maintain their identification with psyche, while men need to actively separate from it and then re-establish a relationship through the anima. This then becomes a separate complex from their predominant masculine ego-complex. In the same way, women establish a rational masculine complex, the animus, that is separate, standing side by side their feminine nature. Both anima and animus provide a balance for the individual between feminine and masculine, feeling and reason, and spirit and nature.

Today these lines are being redrawn, or one could say that they were always fluid and we are now expanding our understanding of the inherent fluidity between the feminine and masculine. The difference between feminine and masculine is not the same as the difference between men and women. The former are psychological states of being while the latter are self-descriptions. As understood in the stages of conscious development and in the myths that expand on these themes, both men and women undergo similar development. The masculine and feminine in each must embark on developing what is needed for that particular aspect of the personality—be it feminine or masculine. Only in this way will we establish wholeness and ignite the transcendent function to give birth the new third element, the child—called *Pleasure* in the myth of Amor and Psyche.

ENDNOTES

[1] Chrétien de Troyes, (1182-1190). *Perceval ou le Count du Graal.*

CHAPTER IX

Analysis of The Nature and Source of Creativity: *Creative Man, Art and the Creative Unconscious, The Place of Creation*

Neumann was especially interested in creativity and wrote extensively about it in his many books. *Creative Man: Five Essays*, includes chapters on Kafka's *The Trial*, poet Georg Trakl, Chagall 's illustrated Bible, Freud, and Jung. Another of his books, *Art and the Creative Unconscious*, includes chapters titled: "Leonardo da Vinci and the Mother Archetype"; "Art and Time"; "A Note on Marc Chagall"; and "Creative Man and Transformation." He wrote a book analyzing the archetypes found in art, *The Archetypal World of Henry Moore*. And Neumann's exceptional book, *The Place of Creation*, examines the meta-psychological and transformational aspects of creativity. The other aspect of his interest in creativity is Judaism, particularly its mystical side, which we discussed in an earlier chapter.

Neumann studied many superb creative writers, artists and composers: Rembrandt, El Greco, Henri Matisse, Vincent Van Gogh, Paul Gauguin, Paul Klee, Paul Cézanne, Pablo Picasso, Salvador Dalí, Hieronymus Bosch, Richard Wagner, Ludwig van Beethoven, Rainer Maria Rilke, Johann Wolfgang von Goethe, James Joyce, Marcel Proust, Fyodor Dostoyevsky, Thomas Mann, and Herman Melville. He had a particular interest in the work of Franz Kafka. He wrote psychological interpretations of many of Kafka's stories when he was in college. Unfortunately only the one on *The Trial* is published. In these studies, Neumann focused on the essence of creation: from where it emerges, how it expresses itself, and its great value for the world. He looked at each artist's work and life to see beyond what was created. He examined the process, the artist's state of mind, and the effect on the artist and audience. His analysis began with healthy development, then explanation of the neurotic and creative person and their similarities. Neumann explained how important creative individuals are for a healthy collective society:

> Man as *homo creator* is the decisive concern of our times, and whether he can be restored to health and continue to evolve will depend on whether the individual comes once more to experience himself as creative, that is, in touch with his own being and the being of the world. (1989, p. xi)

Art and all aspects of creative expression arise from the archetypes, which are the formless psychic structures of the collective unconscious. Not only art but religion, mythology, rituals, social organization, and consciousness arise from the psyche and become visible expressions of the archetypal energies. Art was apparent from the beginning of human existence as seen in the etching and painting of images on cave walls. The creative impulse gives us ideas formed as images that we bring into material reality. As gifts from the gods, these appear in the form of rituals and cultural canons. It is important to maintain a human transpersonal relationship to be able to hear the gods, ancestors, and voices from the realm beyond where wisdom and knowledge flow into the world.

Societies are established through the wisdom of *Great Individuals,* who are the conduits between the world of reality and the transpersonal. These are the prophets of old and of today. The voices and impulses of these creative individuals illuminate new constellations of the collective unconscious. Yet, as Neumann pointed out, "the same constellations may appear in Great Individuals and in borderline cases of neurosis and insanity" (Neumann, 1974, p.90, n. 2). It is easy to dismiss the revolutionary, or new ideas and ways of being, as a threat to the current social order. But there is a time when the old must die to bring forth the new dawn, a healthier order. We do this individually all the time by remaining flexible and alert to the glimpses of what is new and moving in the unconscious. This is why we pay attention to our dreams. It is *Mercurius* in motion that rarely stops. Most of us can ignore these radical or big changes but not the creative individuals. Neumann referenced the artist Hieronymus Bosh when he observed:

> Intense conflict governed the work of Bosch, one of the most magnificent painters ever to have announced the coming of a new era. He clung consciously to the old medieval canon, but beneath his hand the world transformed itself. It became demonic and gnostic...temptation...in the paranoiac despair of his ascetic, medieval consciousness he experienced the revival of the earth archetype around him, glittering demonically in every color. (1974, p. 95)

From the Middle Ages to the Renaissance and French Revolution the social canon shifted radically. The archetype moved from the spiritual pole back to the earth archetype. Suffering the static nature and poverty of a well-established culture will cause the pendulum to shift in the opposite direction to bring what is missing into reality. A new force will break through in art, literature, music, science and politics. The creative individuals bring across sparks from the unconscious that help renew the spirit of the time—change is continuous via the directives of the unconscious. Neumann described three stages the artist goes through in responding to the creative impulse from within: 1. self-expression of the unconscious; 2. representation of the cultural canon; and 3. compensation for the cultural canon depicting art outside of time. It is here the artist is truly alone with the primal creative force: "We begin to see that the supreme alchemical transformation of art merely reflects the alchemical transformation of the Great Individual's personality" (Neumann, 1959, p. 104). Further:

> The principle functions of all art is precisely to set in motion the archetypal reality of the transpersonal within the individual and on the highest level of artist experience to bring the individual himself [or herself] to transcendence—that is, to raise him [or her] above time and epoch. (1974, p. 106)

Through history, the artist becomes less identified with the collective and more individualized. This is the beginning of individuation. Allowing for transcendence and timelessness, a sense of eternity can emerge in the work of art. Understanding world art requires historical knowledge to be able to appreciate cultural differences, for example the symbols in Meso-american or Egyptian art. This allows us to appreciate the timelessness in art. The disintegration of the cultural canon and increasing collectivization leads to the collapse of the social structure, reflecting what happens when an individual loses his or her own world values. There is a collapse into isolation and alienation which Neumann believed had been the case for the prior 100 years at the time of the publication of his paper "Art and Time" in 1951. We certainly see this all around us today. As Neumann emphasized:

> When the world of security crumbles, man is inevitably devoured by *nigredo*, the blackness and chaos of the *prima materia*, and the two great archetypal figures of the Devil and the Terrible Great Mother dominate the world. The Devil is shadow, evil, depression, darkening of the light, harsh dissonance. Elsewhere I have discussed at greater length this incursion of the dark aspect into the Western world and, to the displeasure of those who like to see the world through rose-colored glasses, attempted to draw its ethical consequences....Hell has been let loose and, as in the painting of Bosch, people our reality. (1974, p. 113)

Interestingly, this time in history is also when psychoanalysis entered the picture and the individual focus turned inward, away from the known world. "The rediscovery of the individual is an essential nucleus of creative activity in human civilization" (Neumann, 1979, p. 251). Neumann discussed Surrealism and Impressionism, where the form of the outside world has shattered:

> All these artists suffer the demonic violence of the inward power. Whether they ae driven like Munch into solitude and sickness, like Van Gogh into the release of madness, like Gauguin to the distant isles of primitivism, or like Picasso into the amorphous world of inner transformation, their despair and the strain under which they work contrast sharply with the tranquility of earlier artists, who felt they were carrying on a tradition. (1974, p. 117)

This leads to a dehumanization of art. The psychic symbol takes over. Chaos rules. But it is only here that the new world vision breaks through, in compensation for the materialism dominating our outer view of the world—and the decay of our cultural canon and personal values. In response, the collective unconscious awakens. We are faced with the void at the center, which happens to be both chaos and transformation. As Neumann explains:

> It is the dissolution of a world out of joint, a world whose whole soil is shot through with volcanic crevices; the norms collapse, floods of lava destroy the existing order, but geysers of creativity spurt from the tortured soil. For in this very dissolution a deeper plane of reality is disclosed, yielding its secret to those who, torn like the world itself, experience its primordial psychic source, which is also their own. The divine and the human travel the same road, the world and man are not a duality of one confronting the other; they are an inseparable unity. The moon rises in the soul of every individual, and the house in whose forehead the eye of the godhead opens is you yourself. (1974, p. 147)

In *Creative Man*, Neumann's lifelong friend, Gerhard Adler, noted that, "Neumann built a bridge between the personalistic genetic view and the transpersonal archetypal aspects of the psyche....his work did not spring from his intellect but from a deep and living contact with the unconsciousness sources of creativity" (Neumann, 1979, p. XV). Reading

Neumann's material, it becomes clear that he experienced the transpersonal, the unitary reality. He wrote from experience, not speculation.

When the wound opens up—and it can in a psychic eruption when one struggles with the complexes and shadow that torment a life—one is more than an ego facing the outer world. Rather, one resides near the internal waters of life that fructify and offer up imagination and creative sparks, opening up new ways to see the world and solve its problems. It is that eye of the godhead that took its place in Neumann's forehead in his vision and continues to take its place in ours, if we open to it. Neumann reminded us that, "Rigidity and chaos...are directly opposed to the creative principle, which encompasses transformation" (1974, p. 163). Through images both inner and outer, a new wholeness emerges and brings with it the creative spark. "The development of the intrinsically unknown substance, of the intrinsically unknown and unrepresentable one world, brings with it a confrontation and a differentiation" (1974, p. 174). In other words, the unitary symbol is separated into two: one inner and one outer. To clarify, the tree outside that we see with our eyes is just as much of an image as the symbolic tree we create from inside our mind/psyche. Here is where the categories of *being* (the tree outside) and *meaning* (the tree inside) coincide. As Neumann points out, "When things, a landscape or a work of art come alive or 'grow transparent,' this signified that they are transformed in what we have called 'unitary reality'" (1974, p. 175). This unitary reality is the experience beyond the outer image that moves us to meaning. "The creative process is synthetic, precisely in that the transpersonal, i.e., the eternal, and the personal, i.e., the ephemeral, merge, and something utterly unique happens" (1974, p. 189). It becomes an experience. This is the transcendent function that Jung talks about. Neumann succinctly concluded:

> The rapture of the flowing deathlessness of creativity is just as much at work in man as in nature; indeed, it is only in his creative flowing that man becomes a part of nature, is joined once more to the "one reality" of existence, in which no enduring thing can endure, because all is transformation." (1974, p. 202)

The concept of the unitary reality signifies the original undifferentiated wholeness that we were all steeped in after birth, living in the maternal uroboros. "...the rolling wheel of eternity...the creative point of existence as pure present, both turning and at rest" (Neumann, 1974, p. 203). There was not a separation into opposites, instead all opposites blended into one mass. Through the process of centroversion, the psychic pieces begin to differentiate and separate out leading to the development of the ego-Self axis, where inner and outer become distinct. Neumann used the ego-Self axis to explain how the creative flow from the unconscious flows through the axis into the world of the ego. The world of matter and reality is pierced by images that offer us access to the affective experience of the beyond and a part of the Self. Here creative life flows in and out, as in an *I-Thou* relationship, a place of Tao. The ego is expanded and transformed by this experience: "The nature of creativity in the extra-human as well as in the human realm is always the incorporation, that is, the turning into form of what until then had been just formless dynamic energy" (Neumann, 1989, p. 41). More specifically, Neumann described:

> Since the creative process takes place outside of consciousness and must therefore be looked upon as a borderline experience of the ego, any attempt to approach this central and primal vortex is a hazardous undertaking. It is in the very nature of such an undertaking that its object cannot be captured by the direct intervention of consciousness, but that one must seek to approach the center in question by a sort of ritual circling, an approach from many sides. (Neumann, 1949, p. 11)

The formless dynamic energy at the core of this creative process is the eternal problem of the archetype, gaining meaning through image to become a symbolic experience. It speaks to us personally, yet transpersonally to the whole world-soul. In the process, it becomes a revelation of something entirely new. Yet, the creative genius is never possible without the proximity of the devil, who in his (its) capacity as God's shadow, is apparently unable to discriminate between destroying and creating. It's a fine line between the two. What is reflected by this inner dynamism is also projected out to our outer world. We can see these changes clearly in the development over the ages in expressions of art:

> We must face our own problems and our own imperfections; and at the same time we, must integrate a superabundant outward and inward world that is shaped by no canon. This is the conflict which torments modern man, the modern era, and modern art. (Neumann, 1974, p. 131)

The creative individual is different than the average person. The archetypal mother remains important for the creative person, who does not become neurotic from this continuing relationship. He or she must follow the course of normal development through the hero's journey to slay the father and "dethrone the conventional world of the traditional canon, and seek an unknown directing authority, namely the Self that is so hard to experience, the unknown Heavenly Father" (Neumann, 1974, p. 185). It is the realm of the archetypal mother that constellates the creative process. Yet remaining connected to her realm, the unconscious, results in great suffering as the personal complexes are always connected to the potency of the archetypes, resulting in unconscious existential suffering. The creative individual lives with the reality of life and death, which is nature's rhythm.

Transformation is the result of recovery from illness as well as the mystical loss of consciousness in ecstasy. The individual may be changed permanently, while a partial change may result from a neurotic's change in behavior, or conscious attitude. This increased consciousness is significant but from depth psychology we know "that unless this change goes hand in hand with a change in the unconscious components of the personality, they do not amount to much" (Neumann, 1974, p. 151). It is important to change the complexes— inferiority or mother, for example— which are the unconscious elements linked to archetypes with which we struggle. A change in intellectual orientation is limited to consciousness and does not impact the complexes linked to the deeper layers from where our behaviors and affects emerge. What is needed is a crack in the tight ego control of the intellect. This is so common today where the world exists only as a reflection of the ego and nothing more. But when this cracks, there can be an irruption from the unconscious. The seriousness depends on the degree of tension between consciousness and the unconscious. One can oftentimes feel this coming—something loosening in the personality—or it can feel totally alien. These experiences accompany the stages of life which are always transformative. The process of growth or rebirth can be helped along with accompanying rituals that are connected to each phase. Unfortunately, we no longer have these rituals. We, therefore, must endure the shock and suffering of transformation on our own, which unfortunately results in high levels of depression and youthful suicide that we are now seeing. Neumann remarked:

> Domination by our one-sided culture of consciousness had led the individual almost to a sclerosis of consciousness; he has become well-nigh incapable of psychic transformation. In this situation the ego becomes an exclusive ego, a development reflected in such terms as "egoistic" and "egocentric." It becomes closed both to the *thou* of the self, of the individual's own wholeness, and to the *thou* of the outside, of the world and mankind. (Neumann, 1974, p. 160)

What results from this is a dangerous tension of opposites and repression, which is a destructive emotional charge that can erupt from the shadow. The two sides of the Devil are rigidity and chaos. Both are opposed to the creative principle. When the door to the unconscious is shut, we have an irruptive possession. When it remains open, the creative transformation is related to the Self. This allows the power of the creative to present itself in the form of new symbolic reality that is more complete than conscious reality alone. Neumann pointed out that we pay a high price for the sharp focus of our intellect and rational conscious knowledge. We believe that is the pinnacle of humanity. In fact, it causes a destructive split in the one world, inside and outside, psyche and the perceived world. When the ego senses it is not alone—that there is another force far greater than it—perhaps because of illness or an irruption from the unconscious, then a tension develops. What we learn in the process is that the unconscious has a will of its own. We need to hold the tension of the two poles: a more stable ego consciousness and a super-charged unconscious. The only way to do this is to endure the suffering of not knowing, being alone and afraid, going mad. But that is when the transcendent function comes into play and reveals the unifying symbol that bridges, transcends and surpasses the opposite sides of the personality. A new creation, a new third position is revealed that resolves the horrible tension. The personality is now reborn into the unitary reality. Hopefully it is lasting. This is the total world of transformation that the creative person experiences for him or herself and for the collective that is all of us.

I have selected a few images to describe that reflect this dynamism between the two realms, inner and outer, a view into the unitary reality Neumann so beautifully described.

Dylan's self-portrait

Dylan's self-portrait: A self-portrait a five-year old girl has painted. Her head looks straight ahead with one large eye in the center of her forehead, her hair covering the side of her face. One feels that she still has the view back into the prenatal world of absolute knowledge with one eye that looks in and out. Here she is seeing more than merely our reality plane even though she looks straight ahead. The experience transcends inner and outer, as it does in Leonardo da Vinci's paintings.

Leonardo da Vinci's Mona Lisa

2. Leonardo da Vinci's Mona Lisa: The world of matter becomes so mundane while the light emerges from behind as well as through the skin, flooding the painting with a feeling of the world beyond. The slight smile on the face suggests an unspoken joy or knowing. The eyes gaze out while at the same time focused inward, expressing that which is wholly other of the unitary reality. "A great work of art could not move every one of us if an "everyman" was not at work within the individual artist" (Neumann, 1974 p. 115). "We can follow this phenomenon very clearly if we observe the process of individuation...and study the creative productions, symbols, and sequences of active imagination that emerge as this process unfolds" (1974, p. 123).

Van Gogh

3. Van Gogh offers another example of the experience of this unitary reality captured in image. His paintings move and vibrate as if a secret wind is blowing past, taking them from outer reality into a deeper reality. At the same time, they glow with rich colors that glisten from an inner light. Many of his paintings are simple wheat fields, images taken from reality but transformed into much more. We can feel the painter's transcendent experience and view into another energetic dimension through his rendering.

Mark Rothko

4. Mark Rothko's paintings are an example of modern art, where all elements of the world of the ego are completely broken down. What remains is the fluid shape of color that vibrates and deepens as you sit with it. It becomes an emotional, ecstatic experience, otherworldly and of the world of the psyche. If you have ever been to the Rothko Chapel in Houston, you would have the exceptional experience of feeling the spirit come though his very contemporary art in a moving way. Unfortunately, Rothko committed suicide as one who fell too deeply into the creative nexus. With both the paintings of Rothko and Van Gogh, the viewer is taken on a journey to the edges of the unitary reality.

Henry Moore

5. Henry Moore is one of Neumann's favorites. Three sculptures show how Moore's work changes. One is somewhat representational, depicting the family unit through his creative process. Another is creation of a mother-child dyad that is merely an indication of the two, leaving it to our imagination to complete the image or to see the form in a new way. The third is a complete departure from reality, revealing an abstract dyad with a view through the center void into what is beyond—very much pointing to an inner-outer view. As Neumann clarified, "A basic feature of all modern art is its striving to get back to the archaic again, to the original source beyond our differentiated modern consciousness" (Neumann, 1985 p. 43).

Andy Warhol's Self portrait

6. Andy Warhol's art is a different genre and goes to the far extreme of anti-spiritualism. It can be seen as a commentary on the anti-humanist direction our world has moved into. His art is made to create a sense of nothing but the materialistic, flat features of a vacant, meaningless pop world. The tomato cans and cola bottles are icons of our materialistic world but Warhol's portraits painted at the end of his life cannot hide the deeper emotion and a further dimension behind the flat illustration.

These examples show the movement of art, "the cutoffness of modern ego-centered people living in a partial reality with the experience of meaningless" (Neumann, 1989 p. 205). "The normal ego is generally rigid while the creative human crosses boundaries to pierce through to the creative nature of reality, and to grasp its essence and shape it into artistic form" (1989 p. 138). The form reflects our culture. Still pertinent to us today, Neumann said:

> Times of peril pass, totalitarian states fall just as democracies do; what remains is man [humankind], forever changing and creative; the transformations of his consciousness merely demonstrate the invincibility of the human psyche, which transcends the old, destroying it that it may be reborn in a new form. (1989 p. 229)

It is quite apparent that outside of any intentional conscious process, the psyche continues to impact us in a very significant way. The shadow is always present, acknowledged or not.

CHAPTER X
On the Paper "Mystical Man"

As part of his interest in creativity and in the healthy development of the personality, Neumann took an interest in the mystical, and the process that leads to such an experience. We may say the mystical has an affinity with religion but it is more than that. It is the unique interest that our species has for creating meaning. We strive to understand the world around us and our place in this cycle of never-ending events and time. This is a phenomenon unique to *Homo Sapiens.* It is evident from the earliest cave paintings where humans strove to capture images of their world, animals, and the sky. It was a depiction of the outer world but clearly also a reflection of their inner world—a wonderful interplay of both. As we know, rituals developed to honor that unknown force that seemed to be able to maintain the world in a predictable state. Humans believed they could influence the *gods,* as this force became known, by honoring them with sacrifices and tribute. Religions developed and became more and more complex, all the while maintaining the singular essential belief that the transpersonal force in our world needs attention and reciprocal relationship.

Psychologically, this is the development of the ego-Self axis, a relationship of the inner world of psyche with the outer world of nature and culture. We call this interest in the emanations of the unconscious: mystical. "For us the mystical is rather a fundamental category of human experience which, psychologically speaking, manifests itself wherever the consciousness is not yet, or is no longer, effectively centered around the ego" (Neumann, 1949, p. 12). This can be seen in the experience of *participation mystique*, when no *I-Thou* relationship has yet been established, and the world is still in a state of perfection. This, of course, was before the *Fall* in Genesis: the mistake that humans of all cultures make, the one that makes us human. This forces us to suffer and embark on the hero's journey to learn to stand up against the forces of the inner world that threaten to overwhelm us. In response, we learn to take a stand in the outer world with our own voice and newly discovered authority. "The encounter with the numinous constitutes the 'other side' of the development of consciousness, and is by nature 'mystical'" (Neumann, 1949, p. 14). It is his or her creative Self. In the process of creativity, the ego cannot cling to perceived reality but must expose itself to the chaos of the unconsciousness. Growth and transformation always involve suffering.

These experiences are described as numinous, an epiphany, a revelation or an inspiration. These words describe the mystical. Not only did religions emerge from the mystical but art and morality. The numinous is the *wholly other*. The encounter between ego and non-ego frequently produces a transformation, when it doesn't drop someone into a psychotic episode, which we so frequently see these days. It can be overwhelming to the individual or life changing. Perhaps this begins to explain why so many artists end up taking their own lives. It is the creative void that stands at the center of this experience. It can release its creative force or devour into nothingness. The questions raised by this encounter are: life or death? Sanity or madness? Who am I? The personality can be changed in a flash by an experience of religion, love, artistic inspiration, poetry, a great idea—or a delusion. It is up to the ego to decide how to process this experience. And hopefully the ego is strongly established enough to be able to do so. "Human development...moves towards extension of consciousness and strengthening of the ego; but on the other hand, it requires the mystical phenomenon, the creative process inherent in the transforming encounter between the ego and the non-ego" (Neumann, 1949, p. 19).

Neumann pointed out that this creative-mystical experience is always opposed to the collective values and the dominant religion. It reflects the voice of the Self—opposing the voice of the ego, with its conforming views influenced by its culture. If it speaks, there is a need that it do so. We know this from working with dreams where we gather the messages from the psyche leading us to healthier viewpoints. Such mystical experiences are grounded in the archetypes that express our culture and prevailing dogma, so it will be different for each person. Because of this there has been great hostility to these emanations. This has resulted in mystics seeking introversion and solitude, like Nicholas of Flue or Brother Klaus, the patron Saint of Switzerland that Jung wrote about. He sought through mysticism the heightened tension between the synthesis of the ego and the Self. If anyone has had such an experience, one knows how difficult this is to maintain.

We are now entering a time when psychedelics are becoming more researched and used in the field of mental health. They have played a role in mysticism for thousands of years in religious rituals as a way of opening the door to visions of the transpersonal, the gods and the unconscious. Substances such as psilocybin mushrooms were used in Mesoamerica to open oneself to visions. Sacrificial bleeding through piercings was another way of creating so much pain for the body that it spontaneously opened one to the visionary experience. These techniques were an invitation for *the vision serpent* to engage. Many religions use substances, torture of the body, dance trance, or drumming to enter the realm of visions and the unconscious.

We certainly remember those days in the 1960s and '70s when psychedelics were popular and easily obtainable. *Turn on, tune in, drop out*, as Timothy Leary advised. Many did with both positive and negative results. Now they are being researched for their ability to: open up a person's mind to a new experience of life; broaden their view of what caused their depression or anxiety; release themselves from PTSD experiences by reimagining their experience; or facilitate finding a new way to accept their imminent end of life. These hoped for experiences are mystical and life changing. While they do not occur spontaneously, they can be healing. They open the door to the unknown world that is much larger and more powerful than the ego could ever imagine by causing a change in the personality, as well as a parallel change in the ego and consciousness. Using these substances in the presence of a trained therapist is crucial to prevent psychosis or the ego shutting off in an unhealthy way. While in the recent past there were no trained therapists, further back there were many with experiences of dipping into the creative realm. One example that comes to mind is the vision in *Black Elk Speaks*.

He was surrounded by medicine men and shamans who knew what he was going through and valued his visions for their culture.

Today this mysticism is placed outside of religion for the most part, without the tradition and container that has been passed on for millennia. We are frequently on our own to process these emanations from the psyche and make sense of them. They still emerge and transform the individual. It is the way the system works and it will not be blocked off by a defensive ego. It is more powerful than that. Childhood is a period of mystical experiences because the child personality without a solid ego is still exposed to the transpersonal world. During this period, we see drawings with mandala motifs, circles and swirls across endless pages of drawing paper. Only later are these archetypal experiences projected into the environment (Neumann, 1949, p. 29).

It is also during later adolescence or the early 20s that some get lost in their mystical experiences and hospitalized for psychosis. The hospitalization is the traumatic event, not the experience itself. These youngsters recover and may never have another such episode but live a more fragile creative life. Their development of the ego-Self axis was hindered and for many it is difficult to find their way back. "The reunion with the Self, that is, individuation, is possible only if, instead of regressively dissolving, the ego fully carries out its destined part. The ego is prepared to fight the dragon only after accepting the world's split and conflict" (Neumann, 1949, p. 34). This is very difficult if the person has a weak ego to begin with. For some, it is safer to remain somewhat defended against the unconscious, which tends to flood in too easily:

> Only in the integrated man, who is attached to the center which is his own creative center and which he experiences as the creative center of the world, can the circle close; that circle is peace. For this illumined man the world is transparent and one. (Neumann, 1949, p. 45)

Here the mandalas reflect the archetype of wholeness: the coming together of everything in a state of clear vision with an accepting heart.

CHAPTER XI
Conclusion—Final Thoughts

Erich Neumann's opus is rich, well-conceived and as pertinent to our world today as it was when he developed his theories on psychological human development. I have presented themes, contents and explanations as a useful synopsis of the extensive material. The intention is to generate interest, increase the understanding of his ideas and concepts, and encourage the reader to go back to the original texts. There one can experience first-hand the depth, breadth and continuing significance of his ideas.

The fullness of his understanding of human psychological development of consciousness was profound. He demonstrated how changes in the individual impact larger cultural shifts as he witnessed during WWII—and similar to what we are witnessing now in our world. These are times in our history where we seem to lose an understanding of the impact of the unconscious. Neumann's works lead us back to our ground of being, where we live with opposites that are fiercely alive, impacting our lives and cultures. His writings are comprehensive, clear and steeped in deeply felt experiences that help to place us on firm ground.

As many of his themes and concepts are universal—beginning with archetypes, myths, and images—this book is not only pertinent to Jungian psychotherapists. Anyone interested in understanding the profundity of human nature and its development toward either wholeness or psychosis may benefit. Both the universal and minutiae are herein: from the sky of consciousness to the underworld of the unconscious—and everything in between.

I would like to end with a quote from Erich Neumann's book, *The Place of Creation*, that speaks to a dilemma we are witnessing today. The splitting of the opposites through a shallowness that does not recognize the unconscious even though its effects are everywhere: the internet and social media, ChatBots, virtual reality, and political schisms. Neumann reminded us there is always the possibility for clarity and wholeness:

> Man is always more than an atomized ego, and industrial development and specialization cannot rob him of his innate creativity. Even in the state of stultification and numbness imposed upon him, yes, even when his personality is apparently obliterated, the personality simply withdraws into a secret core of which it itself may be unaware. In the secrecy of the unconscious, future liberation is prepared. Yet even during this waiting period man's awareness of and insight into his true being and the true being of the world persist; they remain a possibility to be experienced in the presentness of the fulfilled moment. (1989, pp. 218-219)

APPENDIX
List of Erich Neumann's Lectures at Eranos in Switzerland

1948 Mystical Man
1949 Die mythishe Welt und der Einzelne
1949 Uber Der Mond und das matriarchale Bewusstsein
1950 Zur psychologishen Bedeuting des Ritus
1951 Kunzt und Zeit
1952 Die Psyche und die Wandlung der Wirklichkeitsebenen
1953 Die Bedeutung des Erdarchetyps für die Neuzeit
1954 Der schöpferische Mensch und die Wandlung
1955 Die Erfahrung der Einheitswirklichkeit und die Sympathie der Dinge
1956 Der schöpferische Mensch und die „grosse Erfahrung"
1957 Die Sinnfrage und das Individuum
1958 Frieden als Symbol des Lebens
1959 Das Bild des Menschen in Krise und Erneuerung
1960 Erich Neumann Die Psyche als Ort der Gestaltung
Olga Fröbe-Kapteyn In Memoriam Erich Neumann
Adolf Portmann Zum Gedenken an Erich Neumann
1948 Mystical Man
1949 The Mystical World and the Individual
1950 On the Psychological Meaning of Ritual
1951 Art and Time
1952 The Psyche and the Transformation of the Levels of Reality
1953 The Significance of the Earth Archetype for Modern Times
1954 The Creative Person and Transformation
1955 The Experience of Unitary Reality and the Sympathy of Things
1956 The Creative Person and the Great Experience

1957 The Question of Meaning and the Individual
1958 Peace as a Symbol of Life
1959 The Image of Man in Crisis and Renewal
1960 The Psyche as a Place of Creation
Olga Frobe-Kapteyn in Memory of Erich Neumann
Adolf Portman In Memory of Erich Neumann

References

Alter, R. (2018). The Hebrew Bible: A translation and commentary. New York: W. W. Norton & Co.

Claremont de Castillejo, I. (1974). *Knowing Women: A feminine Psychology.* New York: Harper Colophon Books.

Furlotti, N. (2015). An amplification of the handless maiden fairytale. To be published.

________(2016) A clear and present danger: Narcissism in the era of Donald Trump. L. Cruz & S. Buser (Eds.), Asheville, NC: Chiron Publications.

_________(2017). Encounters with the animal soul: A voice of hope for our precarious world. In *Jung's Red Book for Our Time: Searching for Soul Under Postmodern Conditions.* (Eds: Murray Stein and Thomas Artz). Ashville, North Carolina: Chiron Publications.

_________(2017) A clear and present danger: Narcissism in the era of President Trump. L. Cruz & S. Buser (Eds.), Asheville, NC: Chiron Publications.

Furlotti, N & Shalit, E. (2013). Wild cats and crowned snakes: Archetypal agents of feminine initiation. *In The Dream and Its Amplification.* Skiatook, OK: Fisher King Press.

Harding, E. (1979). *The Way of All Women.* New York: Harper Colophon Books.

Hillman, J. (1996) *The soul's code.* NY, NY: Grand Central Publishing.

Hillman, J. (1985). *Anima: Anatomy of a personified notion.* Zurich, Switzerland: Spring Publications.

Jaffé, A. (1989). *From the life and work of C. G. Jung.* Eindiedeln, Switzerland: Daimon Verlag.

Jung, C. G. (1917). "The psychology of the unconscious processes," in C. G. Jung, *Collected papers on analytical psychology.* New York: Moffat, Yard, p. 353.

_________(1952). *Symbols of transformation.* Princeton, NJ: Princeton University Press.

_________(1954). *The development of personality.* Princeton, NJ: Princeton University Press.

_________(1970). After the catastrophe, in *Civilization in transition* (2nd ed.) (R.F. Hull, Trans.). Princeton, NJ: Princeton University Press.

_________(1978a). *Civilization in transition* (2nd ed.) (R. F. Hull, Trans.). Princeton, NJ: Princeton University Press.

_________(1978b). "The state of psychology today", in CW10 pp. 157-173. Princeton, NJ: Princeton University Press.

_________(1989). *Memories, dreams, reflections.* New York, NY: Vintage Books.

_________(1989a). *Psychology and religion: West and east.* (2nd Ed.). Princeton, NJ: Princeton University Press.

_________(1989a. Answer to Job, in *Psychology and religion; West and east.* (2nd Ed.) Princeton, NJ: Princeton University Press.

_________(2009). *The red book.* Princeton, NJ: Princeton University Press.

Jung, C. G. & White, V. (2007). *The Jung-White letters.* A. Lammers & A. Cunningham (Eds.). Princeton, NY: Princeton University Press.

Jung, C. G. & Neumann, E. (2015). *Analytical psychology in exile: The correspondence of C. G. Jung & Erich Neumann.* M. Liebscher (Ed.). Princeton, NJ: Princeton University Press.

Jung, E. (1972). *Anima and animus.* Zurich, Switzerland: Spring Publications.

Loewe, A. (2015). I would like to eat some fruit with you: theological positions in the correspondence between Jung and Neumann. In E. Shalit & M. Stein (Eds.), *Turbulent times, creative minds - Erich Neumann and C.G. Jung in relationship (1933-1960).* Asheville, NC: Chiron.

Meier, C. A. (2003). *Healing dream and ritual: Ancient incubation and modern psychotherapy.* Einsiedeln, Switzerland: Daimon Verlag.

Mendes-Flohr, P. (2015). German *Kultur* and the Discovery of the Unconscious. The Promise and Discontents of the German-Jewish Experience. In E. Shalit & M. Stein (Eds.), *Turbulent times, creative minds - Erich Neumann and CG Jung in relationship (1933-1960)* (p.). Asheville, NC: Chiron.

Neumann, E. (1949) Mystical man. In *Spring, 1961*. (9-49). NY, New York: Analytical Psychological Club of New York.

__________(1966). Narcissism, normal self-formation, and the primary reflection to the mother. In *Spring Jour*nal, p. 99.

__________(1968). Mystical man. In J. Campbell (Ed.). *The mystic vision: Papers from the Eranos yearbooks*. (p. 375-415). Princeton, NJ: Princeton University Press.

__________(1971). *The Origins and history of consciousness*. Princeton, NJ: Princeton University Press.

__________(1971a). *Amor and psyche*: *Psychic Development of the Feminine*. Princeton, NJ: Princeton University Press.

__________(1973). *The child*. (R. Manheim, Trans.). Boston, MA: Shambala.

__________(1974). *Art and the creative unconscious*. Princeton, NJ: Princeton University Press.

__________(1979). *Creative man*, five essays: Kafka, Trakl, Chagall, Freud, Jung. Princeton, NJ: Princeton University Press.

__________(1981). *The great mother*. Princeton, NJ: Princeton University Press.

__________(1985). *The archetypal world of Henry Moore*. NYC, NY: Harper Torchbooks.

__________(1989) *The place of creation*. Princeton, NJ: Princeton University Press.

__________(1990). *Depth psychology and a new ethic*. Boston, MA: Shambala.

__________(1994). *The fear of the feminine and other essays on feminine psychology*. Princeton, NJ: Princeton University Press.

__________(2015). *Jacob and Esau: On the collective symbolism of the brother motif*. (E. Shalit Ed.), Ashville, NC: Chiron Publications.

___________ (2019a). *The roots of Jewish consciousness: Revelation Vol. 1.* (Ed. Ann Lammers). London: Routledge.

___________ (2019b). *The roots of Jewish consciousness: Hasidism, Vol.2* (Ed. Ann Lammers). London: Routledge

Shalit, E. & Stein, M. (2016). *Turbulent times, creative minds - Erich Neumann and C.G. Jung in relationship (1933-1960).* Asheville, NC: Chiron Publications.

Vernon, M. (2011). "A troubled relationship with Freud—and the Nazi." theguardian.com, Carl Jung, part 2.

Von Franz, M-L. (1993). *The Feminine in Fairytales*. Boston: Shambala.

Index

www.ingramcontent.com/pod-product-compliance
Lightning Source LLC
LaVergne TN
LVHW050912210926
848482LV00012B/416
9781685031633